"What perfect timing. This is the [...] was too busy simplifying my life. I [...] voked to action. Well done, Joanne [...]"

"If you're like me, you've probably talked a lot about wanting to slow down, cut back, and simplify. Joanne Heim has gone beyond talking about it to actually living it. If you find yourself living a full life rather than simply living life to the fullest, this book is for you."

"Chock-full of practical and holy counsel from a woman who is as wise as she is charming."

LIVING SIMPLY

JOANNE HEIM

Multnomah® Publishers *Sisters, Oregon*

LIVING SIMPLY
published by Multnomah Publishers, Inc.

© 2006 by Joanne Heim
International Standard Book Number: 1-59052-728-3

Cover design by Brand Navigation

Unless otherwise indicated, Scripture quotations are from:
The Holy Bible, New International Version
© 1973, 1984 by International Bible Society,
used by permission of Zondervan Publishing House
Other Scripture quotations are from:
The Message by Eugene H. Peterson, Copyright © 1993, 1994, 1995, 1996, 2000. Used
by permission of NavPress Publishing Group. All rights reserved.
The Amplified Bible (AMP)
© 1965, 1987 by Zondervan Publishing House.

Multnomah is a trademark of Multnomah Publishers, Inc.,
and is registered in the U.S. Patent and Trademark Office.
The colophon is a trademark of Multnomah Publishers, Inc.

Printed in the United States of America

For information:
MULTNOMAH PUBLISHERS, INC.
601 N LARCH STREET
SISTERS, OREGON 97759

06 07 08 09 10—10 9 8 7 6 5 4 3 2 1 0

Dedication

To my family—
Toben, Audrey, and Emma
and
Dad, Mom, and Kristen.
You mean the world to me.

Table of Contents

Acknowledgments

My mother taught me to write thank-you notes when I received a gift. Every New Year's Day we would watch the Rose Parade and write thank-you notes for all the Christmas presents we'd received: "Dear Grandma, thank you for the new purse. It's so pretty. Love, Joanne."

In the process of working on this book, I have received many gifts for which I owe thanks. Not purses or new pajamas or dolls—but gifts of far greater value.

My friend and agent, Bill Jensen. Thank you. I appreciate your insight, your wisdom, and your encouragement. I'm always so happy when your number comes up on the caller ID, knowing the next hour (at least!) will be fun and give me great ideas for the book, what to read next, a great family activity, and what to make for dinner. I'm so glad you are my friend.

To my editor, Steffany Woolsey. Thank you for your encouragement and guidance in this process. What a delight it has been to find a "kindred spirit" in the midst of working together. It's wonderful to discover someone who understands the simple pleasure of an afternoon spent at Green Gables.

My mother and my sister, Kay Friedenstein and Kristen Haufschild. Thank you for being a sounding board for me— the afternoon we spent sitting in the living room and talking through the manuscript helped get me past a stuck spot. And thanks for asking how the writing was going—it helped me sit down and write, knowing you would ask!

My friends, Sarah, Emily, Michelle, and Terri—to name a few. Thank you for your willingness to listen to me talk about this all the time, to pray for me, to offer your ideas and encouragement and prayers. I'm blessed to know you.

The women in my Thursday morning Bible study. Thank you for your prayers for discipline and inspiration—from the time I asked you to pray I noticed a huge difference in my ability to focus and find the time to write. You are faithful friends and I'm so glad to spend each Thursday morning with you.

And last, but by no means least, my family.

My husband, Toben. Thank you for our life together. I wouldn't want to do this with anyone else. I love you.

My children, Audrey and Emma. Thank you for being patient when you heard me say, "Just let me finish this thought...paragraph...sentence." I couldn't have written this without your willingness to "wait just a minute more." And thank you for letting me tell stories about you. Since you probably won't read this until you're older, I hope I didn't write anything to embarrass you!

To Elohim. You are the Mighty Creator. Knowing that this work was "prepared in advance for me to do" was a constant reminder that this is about You and the abundant life You desire for Your children.

*How do we come to choose what it is that we
spend our days doing? Would we choose it again if
we could? Did we choose it today, or has it simply
carried us along somehow?*[1]

ROBERT BENSON

*Make it your ambition to lead a quiet life, to mind
your own business and to work with your hands,
just as we told you, so that your daily life may
win the respect of outsiders.*

1 THESSALONIANS 4:11–12

Choosing Less in a World of More

IF YOU'VE PICKED UP THIS BOOK, CHANCES ARE YOU'RE feeling a little overwhelmed by life. You wish there was less to *do* and more time to *be*. You want to spend more time together as a family but wonder how to fit it in between soccer practice, dance lessons, homework, and babysitting. You desire contentment, but it's difficult to find when everyone around you is upgrading everything—from their televisions to their fall wardrobes. You worry about teaching your kids how to appreciate and care for the things they have when so much around you is disposable.

You think about cutting back, saying no, and choosing less—but it's easy to get caught up in what everyone else is doing. It's hard to be the only one going against the flow.

There's something about the idea of simplicity that tugs at you, draws you in, reveals a longing for something more.

Maybe you're just beginning to think about all of this; maybe it's something you've been pondering for a while. Perhaps you're trapped in the excess, crowded under all the stuff of life; or perhaps you've already begun paring away the clutter to find what the apostle Paul referred to as the "wide-open, spacious life" (2 Corinthians 6:11, *The Message*).

Wherever you are on the journey to simplicity, grab a cup of coffee, get comfortable, and let's walk a little together.

I saw the angel in the marble and
carved until I set him free.
MICHELANGELO

Simple Abundance

ALMOST EVERY DAY I HAVE A CONVERSATION WITH another woman about simplifying our lives. You name it, and we're filled to overflowing.

With kids, husbands, teachers, coaches, and friends, our lives are full. With soccer on Monday, dance on Tuesday, piano on Wednesday, karate on Thursday, and Brownies on Fridays, our schedules are full. With clothes for work, clothes for Saturdays, clothes for church, and clothes for whatever is "in" this season, our closets are full. With toys for the kids, hobbies for us, and sports equipment for our husbands, our homes are full. With backpacks, kids for carpool, bags of groceries, stuff to drop off at school, a bag of things to return to the store, and a meal for that friend who just had a baby, our cars are full.

As mothers, wives, friends, employees, daughters, sisters, aunts, volunteers, leaders, participants, Sunday school teachers, lunch moms, and whatever else—well, you get the picture.

Yes, we want full lives, but this is getting ridiculous.

"This complex, consuming life may be okay for everyone else, but not for us"—that's what one mom said to me the other afternoon at preschool pickup. She and her husband had been talking about how to simplify their lives and scale down from the mass consumption surrounding them. She said it feels like they've been going along with everyone else, without giving it much thought—until one day it got to be too much.

Time for a change.

We've tried more and more of everything, only to find that life hasn't gotten better, easier, or become quite what we hoped it would be. We rush from this to that; we long for the day when life won't be quite so busy.

As Robert Benson writes, "We rush through the present toward some future that is supposed to be better but generally turns out only to be busier."[2]

Ugh. Busier than this?

Instead of finding fulfillment, we feel overwhelmed and pressed for time. An empty day on the calendar is rare; when it does occur, it's "such a treat," as one woman recently said to me. "But instead of just relaxing and enjoying it, I typically use it to catch up on everything I've fallen behind on." And so an empty day becomes overly full and the chance to rest is lost.

Is this the kind of abundant life Jesus really meant when He said, "I have come that they may have life, and have it to the full" (John 10:10)? Does a full life mean rushing madly from here to there, distracted by the thing we've forgotten to put on our to-do list but we know is rattling around *somewhere*? I hope not.

I love *The Message* paraphrase of Jesus' words in John 10:10: "More and better life than they ever dreamed of." We have the more; we're full to the top—but is all this crazy busyness what we dreamed of as little girls? Did our Barbies rush around their Dream Houses worried about getting Skipper to soccer practice on time, burning dinner for Ken, and wishing for life to slow down?

The question I always go back to is this: *When does the better begin?* Because I can dream some pretty amazing dreams. How about you?

A certain passage from Thoreau's *Walden* resonates deeply with me:

Our life is frittered away by detail. Simplify, simplify.

Okay, fair enough. But the quiet space of Walden Pond can be difficult to locate in today's busy world.

We've been brought up to believe that God is in the details. Yet the question remains: How do we simplify the details that make up our lives? And aren't those details important?

We read *Little House on the Prairie* to our children and wonder, *Could we have a life like that? Could my family ever live so simply and be so happy?*

We've become accustomed to more; we imagine that we might be bored if we change too much. If we were to place the equivalent of only a shiny penny and a tin cup under the tree on Christmas morning, would our kids stage an uprising?

Perhaps, rather, they would find peace. And maybe we would discover a quality of life that's missing from our busy schedules—a different kind of abundance.

And so we wonder if it's time to cut back. We clean out a closet or two, but it doesn't do the trick. We want to get back to the way things used to be, when life was simpler and centered around God and family...but just how do we do that living in today's world? We can't go back in time, and Walden's not on my local map.

After spending four college years majoring in home economics, my mother says the thing she remembers most is this: *Simplicity is the key to good design.* Whether you're designing an outfit, a room, a house, a meal, a party, an invitation, or even a life, simplicity is what makes it work.

I'll be honest: Some of my desire for a simpler life came as a result of circumstance rather than choice. My husband took a new job and our family moved from Colorado to Southern California; we had no choice but to downsize.

Our house here is less than half the size of our old one. It seemed easier to decide that downsizing was something we were choosing to do. *Just keep telling yourself that, Joanne,* I would think as I added each new armload of stuff to the garage sale pile.

So we ruthlessly sorted through everything we owned. Then we threw a monster garage sale and sold off five rooms' worth of furniture, toys, knick-knacks, baby toys, and clothes. Finally, we packed the rest in boxes and headed west.

We *still* had too much stuff.

For the first month or two after moving to San Diego, I took at least one box a week to the Goodwill drop-off. (Goodbye, sweaters, winter coats, ski rack, and more toys and clothes!) Finally, after employing some creative storage solutions, the car fit in the garage.

The good news? Everything left is stuff we *really* like.

The bad news is that once we got settled and made some new friends, our lives were still too full for comfort. It was like the feeling you get after Thanksgiving dinner when you realize you shouldn't have had that second helping of stuffing or the pecan *and* pumpkin pie. Everything is good; it's just too much, and you're left feeling too full to move comfortably.

And so I've found that living a simple life is more than just getting rid of stuff. Stuff is part of it, for sure. But it's also about full calendars, schedules, commitments, activities, and to-do lists. Like Thanksgiving dinner, a lot of it is good—nice things, people we enjoy, and activities we really do want to do. But we're too full—stuffed, in fact—and we feel a little sick knowing we just can't handle all those things our lives are full of.

So what are we to do?

Consumed By an All-Consuming Life

In our defense, we're conditioned to be consumers.

We're trained to want more in order to be happy, starting with the commercials we see during Saturday morning cartoons. From Strawberry Shortcake dolls to Easy-Bake Ovens, we're always just one purchase shy of complete and utter happiness.

As children, we watched those kids on commercials having the time of their lives with their new Slip 'n' Slide. We thought we could buy that kind of happiness, too—for only $9.95! Life would be better; spelling tests would be easier; the schoolyard bully would leave us alone.

Things haven't changed much. Substitute an Ab Lounger and a Magic Bullet for the doll and oven, and we're still just one possession short of complete happiness. Life would be better; kitchen clean-up would be a snap; other people would *like* us more.

It hardly seems to matter if it's something we need or even want. We must have it—because it's there.

I love the episode of *Veggie Tales* when a discontented

Madame Blueberry discovers Stuff Mart. The singing vegetables promise her, "All you need is lots more stuff!" Her unhappiness, they insist, stems from not having the right kinds of stuff. So she quite literally buys into the message. It's only when her too-full house begins to topple beneath the weight of her purchases that she realizes there really *is* such a thing as too much stuff.

Even though we know in our heads that finding happiness in stuff isn't possible, the message that "all you need is lots more stuff" prevails. The Madame Blueberries of this world just can't compete with the world's insistence that stuff is the way to go. So we fill up our lives with things we don't really need or want until, like Madame Blueberry's house, the weight of it becomes too much and it all comes crashing down.

☙

My youngest daughter, Emma, recently came running into the kitchen, shouting, "Mom, you've got to come see this! We need this!"

I followed her to the television, expecting to see the latest Barbie or a tool that braids hair and adds beads all in one quick and easy step.

Nope. She was desperate for us to purchase a new food storage system. According to the infomercial, it uses one size lid for all the containers and stores compactly on the pantry shelf.

"We *need* this, Mom," Emma insisted. "It *spins*." (Not what I was expecting from my five-year-old, to say the least!)

Like most of us, I already have a pretty extensive collection of containers for leftovers. But children, it turns out, aren't the only ones who have a hard time determining needs from wants.

I have to remind myself that I have everything I need—and more—on a regular basis. Most of us have more than enough. Some have so much, in fact, that if we are not embarrassed about what we have compared to what others do not, we ought to be.[3]

We have enough to eat, I have plenty of clothes to choose from each morning, and my car starts when I turn the key. On top of that, I have a wonderful family, a great husband, my kids go to a fantastic school, and I'm blessed with terrific friends.

Teaching Audrey and Emma to stop and remember all we have is an almost daily ritual as well. I've found that one of the most effective ways to teach myself (and my daughters) the difference between needs and wants is to be thankful. By thanking God for providing for us, we quickly see just how much He has given us that we don't really need. The things I'm most thankful for didn't come from the mall.

I'm thankful for…

my family
laughter
my eyesight
the way my kids wrap their arms and legs around
    me when I pick them up for a hug
my husband
vibrant colors in nature
the smell of rain
lazy Saturday mornings
the sound of the ocean
that first sip of coffee early in the morning when
    the rest of the house is still sleeping

The list goes on and on.
What are you thankful for?

Instant Anticipation?

Along with wanting to consume more and more, we live in an "instant" society that has shortened our attention spans and encouraged distraction. From instant mashed potatoes to instant coffee, we want what we want, and we want it *now*. We're so conditioned to believe that now is better that we settle for mediocre rather than wait. Let's face it—instant mashed potatoes and instant coffee don't come close to the real thing.

The bottom line is this: We've lost our sense of anticipation, and our lives are poorer for it.

Stop and think about that for a minute.

With credit, we no longer have to save up for a big purchase. As a result, whatever it is we "couldn't live without" loses its appeal almost as soon as we get it home.

With fast food, we no longer have to wait for dinner to simmer on the stove, smelling good smells while our stomachs growl and our mouths water.

When we do have to wait—at a traffic light, in line, on hold—we are instantly impatient. "Come *on*," we mutter under our breaths. (So that's where our kids get it from!)

Because we lack anticipation, we're missing something. We've forgotten that anticipation is half the fun.

The sixteenth-century French writer François Rabelais once said, "For he who can wait, everything comes in time." What are we missing by refusing to wait?

I'm reminded of a line from a song we sing at church: "Strength will rise as we wait upon the Lord." Waiting is a big part of walking with God, and something we chafe against. Telling my children to wait for something is nearly always met with "Awwww!" Waiting is hard.

Unlike our society, which tells us we shouldn't have to wait for anything, the psalms are filled with instruction to wait. We "wait in expectation" for God to answer our prayers (Psalm 5:3;

130:6). We "wait in hope" for the Lord (Psalm 33:20). We "wait patiently" for God to hear us and to act on our behalf (Psalm 37:7, 40:1). We "wait for the Lord and keep his way" while we wait (Psalm 37:34). We "wait," plain and simple, for Him to answer us (Psalm 38:15). We "wait for [His] salvation" (Psalm 119:166).

Indeed, we find instruction to wait throughout Scripture. We wait for deliverance (Proverbs 20:22). We receive blessing when we wait for God (Isaiah 30:18). We're told, "It is good to wait quietly for the salvation of the Lord" (Lamentations 3:26). Hosea tells us to "wait for your God always" (12:6).

In the New Testament, we're still required to wait, but now we wait "eagerly" and in hope with all of creation for the return of our Savior. Paul says, "But if we hope for what we do not yet have, we wait for it patiently" (Romans 8:25).

Patience always reminds me of singing along as a child to *The Music Machine*, a children's musical that taught about the fruits of the Spirit. For some reason the song about patience is the one I remember best—maybe because it's the most difficult lesson to learn. Poor Herbert the snail is always in a hurry and has to learn patience by slowing down. Certainly it's the song we sang most often. (My mother *still* sings it to me over the phone, using an agonizingly slow, droning snail-like voice, when I get in too much of a hurry.) Here are the lyrics:

> Have patience, have patience.
> Don't be in such a hurry.
> When you get impatient,
> you only start to worry.
> Remember, remember,
> that God is patient too.
> And think of all the times when others have to wait for you!
> —Herbert the Snail, *The Music Machine*

I think another reason we don't wait much is because we get distracted so easily. If we have to wait too long, we lose interest and move on to something more immediate. We forgo the food we really want at the mall food court because the line is too long. Commercials take too long, so we even watch two television programs at once. If it's an unavoidable task, we find something else to do simultaneously (applying mascara at the traffic light, anyone?).

And the worst of it is that we reward such behavior by calling it *multitasking*.

Multitasking, I've decided, is not all it's cracked up to be. When I try to "multitask," I find myself putting laundry in the pantry, milk in the closet, and forgetting why I walked down the hall to the bedroom. Do you do the same, or is it just me? (Please tell me you do the same!)

So I've decided to stop. I am *not* going to do six things at once anymore. And while I'm on a roll, I am also going to slow down. I'm going to stop rushing and begin taking my time.

I recently read an article about "the slow movement." Author Carl Honoré had this to say about slowing down:

> Our culture puts a premium on speed, deifying this notion that faster is better, that you must fill every single moment with activity. There's a powerful taboo that makes "slow" a dirty word. In this hyped-up world, we need to keep an eye on our personal speedometers— it's very easy to do things fast just because everything else around you is going fast, without even considering whether or not it makes sense.[4]

I'm going to spend more time thinking about whether speeding through an activity makes sense.

When Audrey sits down to do her homework in a hurry, I

hear myself repeating words my own mother said to me: "If it's worth doing, it's worth doing well."

Sometimes I wonder, *In how many areas of my life am I doing well?* It's a tough question—and one I'd rather not dwell on, because too often my answer is "Not many."

Are we taking the time to do things right the first time? Or are we rushing through life, haphazardly slapping together projects and telling ourselves we'll fix them later?

If it's worth doing, it's worth doing well.

If we're not doing something well, it begs the question, *Is it worth doing in the first place?* If not, then *why* are we doing it in the first place?

Even more important, how will our children learn to do things well if we're not leading by example?

If it's worth doing, it's worth doing well. I can't say it without a smile. Even while I know it to be true, I don't like hearing it any more as an adult than I did as a child. My mother recently confessed that she feels the same: "I hated hearing Mother say it to me!"

Audrey is learning to write in cursive. She's thrilled about it—it's such a big kid thing to do. But she hurries through her worksheets and gets upset when I go back and erase strings of lowercase *E*s and *L*s that flail on the page, drunkenly looping too far above or below the line.

"It's faster in the long run," I tell her, "to take the time to do it right the first time." She sighs and picks up her pencil and sighs again. I give her a squeeze and plant a kiss on top of her head because I know just how she feels.

If it's worth doing, it's worth doing well. Just because it's true doesn't make it fun to hear.

Of course, even though I know it's better to do it right the first time, I don't always follow my own advice. And so I rip out a knitting project, delete an entire page of writing, or refold all the laundry in my armoire.

Why are some things so hard to learn?

Audrey brought home a memory verse last year and we all learned it: "Whatever your hand finds to do, do it with all your might" (Ecclesiastes 9:10). It's easy for me to quote back at her when it's time to sit ("Sit still, Audrey!") and do the homework ("Audrey, it's time to do math—not reading") that's due tomorrow ("You can ride your bike after you're finished").

But it's not so easy for me to put into practice as I clean up the kitchen, talk on the phone, fold laundry, watch *Martha Stewart*, and eat a snack—going from one thing to the next without finishing what I was doing. (And I wonder why it feels like I never get anything done!)

There are days when I get lots of tasks half done, but that leaves me feeling dissatisfied and frustrated. Half done is still undone.

And so I take a deep breath, picture my mother's beautiful face, and tell myself to slow down and do one thing at a time.

And to do it well.

Simplify, Simplify

Choosing less is a daily challenge in Southern California. Everyone here has lots and lots of stuff. From fancy cars to million-dollar houses to huge diamonds, more is definitely the way to go. It's easy to feel like we need a bigger house, newer cars, and more bling just because everyone else does.

We all experience the same challenge, whether we're surrounded by movie stars and mansions or cows and cornfields. The truth is, we live in a culture that values supersizing everything, from French fries to SUVs.

I find myself gravitating to extremes. On the one hand it's tempting to turn my back on culture and go overboard—to get rid of everything and start from scratch. I dream of leaving the land of excess and moving to small-town America, where I imagine life to be so much simpler. Or, as one friend recently suggested, moving to a deserted island, building a hut, and living on bananas and coconuts, à la *Survivor*.

On the other hand, it's easy to romanticize the past and give in to the crazy excess, convinced that it was just easier to live a simple life fifty or one hundred years ago. There weren't rows of restaurants only minutes away, so families ate together every night. There wasn't a mall down the road filled with so many fashionable clothes to bring home and stuff into my already overly full closet. Since I can't go back, I might as well give in to the inevitable excess. Why fight a losing battle?

And so I struggle with myself—wanting to "Simplify, simplify," as Thoreau said, and at the same time wondering how to go back from here. Is it even possible? And in my heart of hearts, I have to admit that—at times—I even like the excess. I like having lots of stuff and I like having lots to do. Sometimes empty quiet can be a little scary.

How could we ever simplify something like Christmas after so many years of crazy excess? I take comfort in the thought that even St. Francis, who wrote so compellingly about simplicity, conceded, "We don't need to plunge into abject poverty when we hear the call to simplify our lives."[5] Moderation is key in everything—even simplicity.

"How?" is the question I hear more than any other as I talk to other women about the overwhelming complexities of our lives. Even more, I want to understand the *why* behind simplicity's call.

Why simplicity?

For me, simplicity is not just about how to cook a month's worth of meals in one day or how to speed clean the whole house in thirty minutes. While those things are great and help manage my life and household, what I'm really longing for is a better *quality* of life—one that values quality over quantity.

I want a life focused more on my family than my to-do list, one that is more concerned with creating memories than being perfect, more excited about life together than activities that pull us apart. I want a life filled with more meaning and less stuff, and I'm finding that simplicity is a means to finding a better quality of life.

Saying "no" to some of the excess means being able to say "yes" to others—and having the energy to pursue those things that have more and lasting value.

⁓

I want a rich, full life, one filled with love, joy, family, friends, memories, laughter—don't you? The stories I love to hear my mother tell are filled with relationships, sights, sounds, smells, morals, lessons learned, and fun. I just can't imagine looking back on my life someday and telling my grandchildren stories about shopping at the mall, or the day I got everything checked off my to-do list.

I think our culture has determined that abundance has to be material stuff, and we have bought into it. We've chased after quantity instead of quality, never stopping to see that an abundance of nothing is still nothing.

The abundant life Jesus talked about has to be in keeping with His character. He Himself had nothing—"no place to lay his head" (Matthew 8:20). The things He emphasized as having the greatest value were loving God and loving others. When put to the test about the most important part of the law, Jesus responded,

> "'Love the Lord your God with all your heart and with all your soul and with all your mind.' This is the first and greatest commandment. And the second is like it: 'Love your neighbor as yourself.'" (Matthew 22:37–39)

Any life He wants us to have abundantly must involve these things, if we desire to stay true to who He is.

This is something I've been thinking about for a while. I was reading through my journal the other day and came across this entry:

2/29/04. I was lying in bed thinking about an abundant life—something Jesus said He came to give us: life, and that we may have life abundantly. That's what I want—that's the crux of it. I want my marriage with T. to be abundant—filled to overflowing with love. I want to parent that way—to have abundant love, joy, patience, time, fun with and for A. & E.

Does abundant/overflowing mean full to the brim with not enough room for more? Or does it mean filled with open space and time for everything? I hope it's the latter. I don't want my life to be hectic and pressed, but rather filled with joy and the things that make it worth living.

I want God to be abundant in my life, too—for His love, presence, and grace not only to be sufficient but to overflow from my life and into the lives of others.

I have lots of stuff and it's not doing the trick. I want God's kind of abundance—an abundance of love, joy, peace, patience, kindness, goodness, faithfulness, gentleness, and self-control.

Setting the Angel Free

I'm fascinated by sculpture. When I worked in Paris for a summer, one of my favorite things to do was wander around the Musée Rodin and then buy lunch at the small café nestled into a corner of the sculpture garden. Located in a stately townhome, the museum is filled with large and small statues chiseled from marble and cast in bronze. I especially loved the series of sculptures by Auguste Rodin and his students of a foot—just a foot, but so incredibly detailed it took my breath away.

But my favorite pieces by far were those that seemed only partially finished: huge pieces of silvery white marble, raw and rough on one side, sitting on a table in a room with light streaming in the open windows. From the rough side they looked like they were set down just as they arrived from the quarry and never touched again. But when I walked around to the other side, I was always amazed to see a figure emerging from the stone—a trapped person slowly being freed, just waiting for the sculptor to come back and remove the rest of the stone that was holding him captive.

I can't comprehend how one goes about making a sculpture like this. Michelangelo once said, "I saw the angel in the marble and carved until I set him free." It sounds so simple: You just hold the chisel like this, give it a little tap like so, and voilà! An angel. The problem is that if you hit the chisel too hard, you have a one-winged angel, and no amount of Gorilla glue is going to make it right again. It's not like you can erase your mistake—paint over it or add a little more clay—and have no one be the wiser.

I think that in some ways, understanding the "how" of simplicity is a lot like freeing the angel from the marble. Our lives are like chunks of marble: often unwieldy, and weighted down by all the stuff we've acquired, commitments we've made, and complexities forced upon us that come from living in a world that never stops.

But the quality of life we search for is in there somewhere, and so we start with the obvious things—getting rid of sharp edges, corners, and conspicuous flaws. We begin to consciously choose less, and in so doing we pare away more of the excess. We learn to say no and begin focusing on those things that bring joy, not stress. As we examine our lives, we focus on what is most important; soon, we begin to see the shape of it in our mind's eye.

As the angel begins to emerge, we work more slowly and carefully, chiseling away those things that rob us of abundant life—until we set free the beautiful angel trapped inside.

I don't have this all figured out, wrapped up neatly in pretty paper and tied with a ribbon. But I'm committed to this idea of simplicity, to finding a better quality of life than the excess the world offers. I want my children to grow up cherishing their memories from childhood, knowing that our life together as a family is centered upon Christ and each other.

The more I journey down this path, the more I'm reminded again of God's way of turning things upside down. The last will be first. The rich will be poor. The least will be the greatest. I'm finding that the more I cut out, the more I simplify my focus, the greater the abundance becomes.

Our lives can hold just so much.
If they're filled with one thing,
they can't be filled with another.
We ought to do a lot of thinking about
what we want to fill them with.[6]

A Simple Life

I LOVE THE *LITTLE HOUSE ON THE PRAIRIE BOOKS.*
My girls and I are currently reading through the series each
night before bed. (I'll go ahead and let you in on our bedtime
ritual—we read by oil lamp. I know it sounds a little nuts, but
it's totally renewed their interest in reading together.) We love
reading about Laura and Mary, Pa and Ma, and seeing the ways
in which their lives are the same as ours—Pa outnumbered by
all his girls, a family dog—and different from ours—they had a
covered wagon rather than an SUV!

Audrey and Emma stop me often while I read, asking me to
explain in more detail how butter comes from milk, or why Mary
and Laura go to school in the summer but not in the winter. I
also like to pause while reading to point out how quickly Laura
and Mary obey their parents and how well they play together!

When she turned seven last summer, Audrey had a *Little House*-themed birthday. My mother bought her a Charlotte doll—a handmade rag doll like the one Laura has in the books—and we bought seasons 1 and 2 of the television program on DVD to watch together.

Since school began this year, we've tried turning off the television during the week at our house. With homework to be done and time to play and unwind, there's not really enough time to watch television after school anyway. And to be honest, there's not really that much on television in the afternoons that I want my kids to watch. So much of it seems mindless and without purpose to me. I must be getting old. Or maybe I'm just getting it right. After all, school days with no television are part of what a simple life looks like for my family. Afternoons feel more open, homework is not rushed, dinner is something we prepare together. We play in the backyard, make time to talk about our days, and get to bed without feeling rushed or overwhelmed.

So we've turned off the television during the week, and most of what we find ourselves watching is old episodes of *Little House on the Prairie* on the weekends. As with reading the stories aloud, it's fun to see how Laura and Mary lived back then. We have conversations about honesty, family, giving, friendship, God, angels, and heaven. If you're looking for something to do as a family, I can't recommend these highly enough.

I'm finding that I enjoy *Little House* as much as I did as a child, and that the appeal I found in it then holds true for my children today. The obvious love of the Ingalls family for one another, their thankful attitudes, and their joy in just being together reach out to grab at my heart. They lived simply and without much in the way of material goods, but treasured beauty and craftsmanship in what they did have. They were rich in so many important ways.

I can't begin to say enough good things about the *Little House on the Prairie* DVDs. My girls love watching them; I love watching them. The episodes have sparked some incredible conversations in our home. If you're looking for a great gift for your kids and a sound choice for family movie night, this series is worth considering.

To tell you the truth, *Little House* is slowly taking over the lives of my friends, too. Our husbands think we're a little nuts and just shake their heads at us. We talk about the moral lesson our kids learned from a particular episode, or a scene we remember as children in *On the Shores of Silver Lake*. We dream of taking mother-daughter road trips following the route the Ingalls family took in their travels west. We sheepishly confess that when faced with a difficult situation we sometimes wonder, *What would Ma do?* (Somehow I doubt our husbands talk about what Pa would think while they watch football together!) Our daughters dress up as Laura Ingalls and want to learn to sing the songs Pa played on his fiddle. Watch out, *Little House* is addictive!

Life in a simpler time has an incredible appeal. It's not just *Little House on the Prairie,* either—it can be found in other charming stories like *Anne of Green Gables, Betsy-Tacy, The Secret Garden, National Velvet, It's a Wonderful Life, Little Women,* and all those other books and movies I can't get enough of. I feel the pull of it and long to immerse myself in a simpler life—one that feels more substantial and of higher quality than what we have today. There's a sense that something is missing—that life today has become a cheap substitute for what they had back then.

It's not just the coziness of living in a one-room cabin on the prairie or making dinner on a wood-burning cookstove (although it does sound like a fun adventure). The greater appeal, rather, is the genuine love and care the families had for one another. They found contentment in the simple joy of spending time with each other, the ties that held their community together, and their awareness of God's blessings in life.

Life for the Ingalls family was simpler in some ways, but a lot harder in others. A fierce hailstorm may be something fun for us to watch and listen to on a warm summer evening; but for them, it could mean destroyed livelihood. Making dinner today is often as easy as popping something into the microwave; for them, it entailed planting and tending a garden, and then storing food for the winter ahead.

So is a simple life an easy life?

Not necessarily. But then, lots of things worth having require work and sacrifice and patience. Not all good things come easily.

What's a Simple Life?

I suppose we could approach it journalistically—let's see what I remember from editing my college newspaper. We'll start with the five Ws—who, what, when, where, why—and the lone H—how.

If you've read this far, you already know the *why* of a simple life. Overwhelmed, overcommitted, too busy to rest—the question could well be, *Why not?* Maybe at this point you're ready to try anything!

Who wants a simple life? I do. Most of the women I talk to agree that a simpler life is something they want, too—even if they're not sure what that is.

That leads us to the next question: *What* does "simple" mean? What does living simply look like?

Well, I know what it is *not*. Living simply is not complicated. Not rushed. It does not leave me feeling drained at the end of the day and drained when I get out of bed the next morning. It does not mean feeling constantly pressed for time, five minutes late for whatever is coming next.

Living simply does not mean feeling like my life is too crowded, my house is too cluttered, and that I rarely get to spend time with my friends. It does not mean having so many appointments and commitments that I'm "too busy" to pitch in to help a friend in need. (While helping a friend is something I'll gladly cancel an appointment for, I don't want to have to deal with the hassle of rearranging my life to jump in when someone needs help. I'd rather my friends know I have time to help, and that asking me to lend a hand won't make them feel guilty.)

Living simply does not mean leaving no margin in my life. It does not mean fearing the unexpected—a sick child, an uninvited guest, or anything else unplanned that makes a demand upon my resources of time, energy, emotion, finances.

Living simply does not mean having so many balls in the air that if I drop one, my life will come crashing down.

When I think of a simple life, I think of a life that is less complicated, roomier, filled with the meaningful rather than the urgent. I think of a life centered around people rather than things. I think of a life that's focused rather than scattered, grounded and stable rather than pulled in too many different directions at once. I think of knowing what God wants me to do—being sure of it—and doing it.

I love how a friend phrased it when we were talking recently about living simply. She said, "For me, a simple life would look something like understanding God's plan for me, being still, knowing that I am where He wants me to be, and just going with it."

So *when* does a simple life begin? Today. You don't have to put it off until tomorrow. Annie Dillard once wrote, "How we spend our day is, of course, how we spend our lives." How are you going to spend today? You can begin living simply now. There's no time like the present to get started. As Mary Poppins so wisely said, "Once begun is half done!"

What does a simple life look like to you? Spend some time thinking about it; then perhaps jot some ideas in the margin.

Perhaps it's easier to start with the things that aren't simple and work from there. Go back to the image of a sculpture and think about those big corners and chunks that keep a simple life from emerging.

I recently asked a group of women what makes their lives complicated. Their answers were varied:

"My schedule—the constant running around."

"All the chores and errands."

"Lack of time in the day."

"Saying yes to everything."

"Managing family schedules."

"My job."

"Managing a complicated home."

"Managing the kids—toys, playdates, ballet, school, homework."

"Juggling what I want to do with what I have to do."

"Overcommitment."

"Checking messages—two cell phones, office line, home line, fax line, five e-mail accounts."

"Clutter."

"Trying to live up to what magazines say my house should look like."

"Keeping the house clean."

"The pressure to please."

"Getting my priorities mixed up."

"Deciding what to cook for dinner every night."

No doubt about it, we feel overwhelmed by our lives. We take comfort in Matthew 5:3, where Jesus says, "You're blessed when you're at the end of your rope" (*The Message*), and figure we must be really, really blessed most days. But we forget to acknowledge the second half of the verse: "With less of you there is more of God and his rule." I confess that instead of turning to God and His rule, I often scramble around the house looking for stuff to braid into a longer piece of rope!

Here's another great quote from Robert Benson. (You'll notice that I quote him a lot. He's a very wise man.)

> Some of the things that regulate our lives are things that we can choose or change. Some are not. What is important is that we look at them from time to time and recognize which things are which, and which things can or should or might be adjusted in ways that help us to balance our lives.[7]

Think again about those things that overwhelm you in your life. Some of them are necessary; others are not. Benson's counsel—"recognize which things are which"—is sound advice; but like much sound advice, it can also be hard to swallow.

I'm reminded of the beginning of the Serenity Prayer:

> God, grant me the serenity
> to accept the things I cannot change,
> the courage to change the things I can,
> and the wisdom to know the difference.[8]

Learning to Listen

At times it seems like this full, crazy life just somehow... happened. That we woke up one morning to find our lives overflowing with too much stuff, too many things to do.

It's like the roof suddenly began to leak, but rather than

fixing it, we spend our days running around, madly setting pots and pans under drips until we can barely navigate the house without tripping over a bucket. We waste precious time and energy searching for more buckets—when what we really need is a whole new roof!

Living a simpler life involves changing our focus.

I love the Mary and Martha story in the Bible, perhaps because my mother is named Mary and her sister is named Martha. Perhaps it's because two biblical sisters found a way to argue even while Jesus was a guest in their house. As the oldest sister in my family, I can relate to Martha's feeling that she's the one doing all the work; and as a woman who loves to entertain, I understand wanting to have everything just so.

I hear Jesus saying to me just as He said to Martha, "[Joanne, Joanne], you are worried and upset about many things" (Luke 10:41). He looks at me and shakes His head, knowing my tendency to be scattered and loving me anyway.

And like Martha, I respond, "Yes, but..." and then rattle off everything I'm in the midst of doing.

I'm learning to focus on one thing at a time—to notice when I'm feeling overwhelmed by all those half-done tasks, to take the time to do them well, to stop for a break when I need one. To ask God for His help and energy. To listen to His counsel on what is really important.

My friend Michelle said, "I just go ahead and tell God everything I'm worried about. I get it off my chest, throw it all in a pile at His feet so I know He's aware of it. Then I can sit and listen."

☙

Listening seems easier when I'm away from my real life. I have enjoyed spending time in monasteries, far away from the mall. A friend of mine is a spiritual director and told me about the benefits she'd found to "getting away with God"—spending focused, extended time praying, reading the Bible, listening for God's voice. I'd been feeling overwhelmed by some circumstances in my life, and the thought of getting away to seek God's presence was just what I needed. I read and read my Bible, seeing things I'd never before noticed. The silence and stillness helped me sort through some of the thoughts and worries that had been clamoring for my attention.

Life in a monastery seems simpler. Sometimes I believe I would have liked to be a nun. (Did I mention that I also love *The Sound of Music*?)

The thought of living separate from the world, surrounded by a community of like-minded people, and enveloped in silence is appealing. To have predetermined times for eating, praying, and working seems easier somehow than keeping up with my schedule.

Yes, the times I have spent on retreat at a monastery stand out in my memory as times of peace, calm, and quiet. There is safety in the order of the day, in the sameness of routine. To live, eat, work, and pray in the same space makes it seem more sacred than the outside world.

But that is not the life to which I have been called. And that answers the question of *where*. A simple life for me has to take place within *my* life—not yours, not my neighbor's, not off somewhere in my imagination.

A Beautiful Life

There are no church bells in my life that tell me when to stop one task and start another. There are no set times to do laundry, shop for groceries, have coffee with a friend, or read to my children.

But God is a God of order, and so there must be an order to my day. Some of it is obvious. We get up and eat breakfast, brush our teeth, pack our lunches. The bus comes at 7:10 to take Audrey to school and drops her off again at 3:30. The children bathe before bedtime, which is at 7:30. Bible study is on Thursday mornings from 8:30 to 11. Ballet class is on Tuesday mornings from 8 to 9. Emma goes to school on Tuesdays and Thursdays from 8:15 to 1:15.

But what about the rest of the time?

I love the prayer of Moses found in Psalm 90:12. "Teach us to number our days aright, that we may gain a heart of wisdom." Yes, indeed. How my spirit rises up to echo his prayer.

The word *number* in this verse means pretty much what you'd think—to count, assign, appoint. Makes me think of schedules and calendars and to-do lists. I'm pretty familiar with all of those; how about you?

But the word *gain* in the Hebrew doesn't mean that when we do number our days correctly, a heart of wisdom automatically appears. The Hebrew word in this verse means to grasp, take hold of, seize. It's active, not at all passive.

We need God to help us number—schedule—our days aright so that we can seize wisdom. If we don't learn this skill, presumably we won't be able to take hold of the wisdom God offers.

Why not? Well, taking possession of something requires energy, for one thing. It makes me think of staking a claim in the Old West. (Here comes *Little House on the Prairie* again.) It was a race to find a good claim, and it required energy and alertness and focus. Pa had to wait and plan in order to stake his claim. And once the claim was secured, he had to work the land and produce a crop to earn the deed to the land.

When we don't number our days aright, we're too busy, too tired, too scattered to pursue wisdom with the determination and energy it requires.

Moses is identified at the beginning of Psalm 90 as "the man of God." What a description. I want to be known as a woman of God, don't you?

In that psalm, Moses gives us some insight into how God teaches us to number our days, ways we can begin to learn what God has to teach us about our busy lives.

"Lord, you have been our dwelling place throughout all generations" (v. 1). My Bible notes tell me that the term *dwelling place* means "refuge." God is where we turn for safety and security. We are at home in Him, comfortable in Him. He is the context for our lives.

Next, Moses acknowledges that God is *El Olam*, the Eternal God: "From everlasting to everlasting you are God" (v. 2). God existed before the mountains were born, and time itself is under His control. God is not bound by time as we are, for "a thousand years in your sight are like a day that has just gone by, or like a watch in the night" (v. 4). If we need to learn how to number our days—lives bound by time—the God who established time is the one to teach us.

Can you imagine not living by a clock? What freedom! Never running out of time, never worried about wasting time, never running late, never showing up too early. (Not that showing up too early happens very often…)

But we are creatures of time by God's design. We are the created, not the Creator; He knows us inside and out. We are bound by time and it passes all too quickly. "Our days…quickly pass, and we fly away" (v. 10).

So what are we to do? What makes the difference to those days as they pass?

Wisdom. Knowing what to do and when to do it. Using what we know to make wise choices and godly decisions.

I love how Moses ends this psalm. He asks God to "satisfy us in the morning with your unfailing love, that we may sing for joy and be glad all our days" (v. 14). When we start the day with God, asking Him to schedule our time and tasks, joy is the result. And days full of gladness and joyful song are what I want—for myself and for my family.

And so we begin our day, confident of God's unfailing love, and ask Him to "establish the work of our hands for us—yes, establish the work of our hands" (v. 17). The Hebrew word for *establish* means "to prepare, to arrange, to order."

I love how this verse reads in the King James Version: "And let the beauty of the Lord our God be upon us: and establish thou the work of our hands upon us; yea, the work of our hands establish thou it."

> Satisfy me each morning with your love and establish the work of my hands today, Lord God. Order my day, arrange the tasks to be accomplished, prepare me for the conversations I'll have. Help me sing for joy as I clean my home, read to my children, spend time with a friend. Number my day aright and help me pursue and grab hold of wisdom.

A beautiful life, lived one day at a time. That's the kind of simple life I long for.

A Simple Focus

How do we live simply? One of the ways we can live simply is to do one thing at a time and know why we are doing it. That's what makes the monastery so appealing. The monks know what they are doing as they move through their day—for they too have work to do. Beds must be made; food must be bought and prepared; laundry must be done. The difference is that they know what they are doing when they do it, and why it must be done.

A man once asked a monk what it is that monks actually do. "We walk and we sit and we eat," was the reply.

"Is that all?"

"Yes, but when we walk, we know we are walking, and when we sit, we know we are sitting, and when we eat, we know we are eating."[9]

Living simply involves intention and purpose. It requires focus. It looks beyond the task at hand to the purpose behind it.

Knowing the purpose can make all the difference. Packing lunches can be another chore to get done in the rush before school, or it can be a task undertaken to provide nourishment and energy for my children so they can learn all there is to learn that day. Cleaning my house can be an item on my to-do list, or it can be done for the purpose of making my home a place my family enjoys.

Living simply involves changing our thinking, looking at our lives from a different perspective. It means stopping to ask myself *why* I am doing something and making choices that reflect my purpose.

                    ↄ

I learned some of the Westminster Catechism as a child—from a little, yellow, stapled-together booklet written in Q&A format. I can still remember going over the questions and answers in the bathtub with my sister when we were small.

Question: "What is the chief purpose of man?"
Answer: "To love God and glorify him forever."

As answers go, it's pretty simple. And from it we learn that simple doesn't always mean easy.

One purpose—many ways of living it out.

The biblical passage called the *Shema* begins in Deuteronomy 6, with Moses reviewing the Law with the people of Israel: "Hear, O Israel, the LORD our God, the LORD is one" (v. 4). God is one, but He reveals Himself in many ways and by many names.

Living simply with one focus may look different for you than it does for me. Living a simple life does not mean living a cookie cutter life. Simple is not boring.

☙

I'm a wife. I'm a mother of two girls, ages seven and five. I'm a writer. I'm a friend. I'm a knitter, a cook, a ballet dancer. What about you?

What is the focus of your life in this season? What are the ways you love God and glorify Him today? How are the choices you're making reflecting that purpose and helping you accomplish the task of bringing God love and glory?

Life is made up of so many choices. If our lives are not simple, it is most likely because of the choices we make. Of course, there are always those things we really *don't* choose, things that throw our lives out of kilter. Big things, like a phone call in the middle of the night with news that we hope is just part of a bad dream. And small things, too, like a child home sick from school or the car breaking down.

But many of the things that complicate our lives in the day-to-day reflect our choices. We say yes when we should have said no. We sign up for an activity knowing the schedule will be tight.

> How do we come to choose what it is that we spend our days doing? Would we choose it again if we could? Did we choose it today, or has it simply carried us along somehow?[10]

These are questions we should stop and ask ourselves from time to time.

The good news is that if we make the choice and don't like it, we can sometimes unmake it; if not, we can remember it, learn from it, and choose differently the next time.

The choice for a simple life is yours to make.

He blesses the home of the righteous.

PROVERBS 3:33

A Simple Home

HOME. THERE'S SOMETHING ABOUT THE WORD THAT
creates yearning in me. I don't know if it's the sound it makes,
the memory it evokes, or simply the ideal it inspires; perhaps
it's all those things rolled together. Whatever it is, the idea of
home makes me glad.

I admit, I am a total homebody. I love to be home—a near
perfect day is one when I don't go anywhere. A weekend spent
almost entirely at home is just about as good as it gets. From
my family and my dog to my antique teacup collection and cherished photographs, my home is filled with my favorite things.
I'm all for adventure, excitement, and exploring, but being at
home is my own version of heaven on earth (especially if I can
stay in my pajamas all day!).

I love our little house. Like Anne Shirley, I think, "Home
and I are such good friends."[11] It's warm and cozy, painted with
touches of red, and filled with such treasured things. I sit in the

living room and gaze around happily, remembering stories about every treasured object I see and delighting in each one. My home reflects who I am—who we are—as a family.

Oh, I love to travel and see new places. To go on new adventures and visit familiar old haunts. But to me, the best thing about a trip is the joy of coming home. There's nothing like seeing the sweet, familiar surroundings, or sliding between the clean sheets of your own bed. Toben laughs at how I run around before we leave home, cleaning and scrubbing and changing the sheets. I get it from my mother, I'm sure! I've always felt strongly that if getting home from a trip is wonderful, being met by a clean house is even better.

I agree completely with the sentiments of these familiar lines:

'Mid pleasures and palaces though we may roam,
Be it ever so humble, there's no place like home;
A charm from the skies seems to hallow us there,
Which sought through the world is ne'er met with
    elsewhere.

An exile from home splendour dazzles in vain,
Oh give me my lowly thatched cottage again;
The birds singing gayly, that came at my call,
Give me them, and that peace of mind dearer than all.[12]

Despite all that, I often hesitate before writing *homemaker* in the occupation space on applications for credit cards, school enrollment forms, or other documents requiring such information. Somehow, "homemaker" sounds like a reluctant admission that I'm not living up to my potential as a college-educated, sophisticated woman of the new millennium (whatever that is).

Wife? Mother? What to write? It seems like there are so many other ways to answer the question. I run through the list in my head and tap the pen impatiently against the paper. *Oh well,* I think, and jot it down.

I wonder why the word *homemaker* sounds so funny to my ears in this day and age. Because when I stop to think about it, making a home is a really cool thing. In fact, the word encompasses much of what I do as a wife and a mother. Our home provides my family a place of refuge and safety, a place for rest and relaxation. Our home is a setting in which we make memories and create our life together.

My family called many different houses *home* while I was growing up, but I regularly dream about one in particular. It sat at the top of a long, steep driveway, at the end of a long, steep cul-de-sac. Our driveway made the perfect sledding hill in wintertime. Kristen and I would race our Flexible Flyers down the cul-de-sac and into the street beyond; then we'd trudge back up the hill, pulling our sleds by their rope handles, and do it all over again. Once we were tired and cold, we'd head inside for hot chocolate and throw our snow clothes in the dryer to warm them up. And when we had drunk our chocolate and blown our noses, outside we'd head again.

The inside of the house was wonderful, too. My closet, which was big enough to play in, sat over the staircase. Part of the closet floor was slanted and carpeted, and we could scoot to the top and slide down. Sometimes at night when I was supposed to be asleep I'd sneak in there with my book, close the door, and turn on the light to read "just one more chapter." (I have fantasies about moving back to Colorado Springs and buying that house so my own children can have the same kinds of memories.)

Home will be the thing my girls remember when they grow up. The standard by which they measure every other place they go. Dorothy in Oz understood the poet, too: *There's no place like home*.

My parents have named their home "The Refuge." The title is carved on a piece of wood, varnished and sturdy, and hangs on a tall pine halfway down their driveway.

I love the idea of naming a home. I've often tried to come up with a name for our little house, but haven't yet found one that's just right.

When we lived in England, it was hard to miss a house's name. I'm not sure why it's more common to name your house if you live in England; perhaps it's left over from the days of manor homes and estates. Whatever the reason, people name their houses. The average-looking little tract home across the street from ours was named "Tara." A far cry from the O'Hara plantation, but that's what it was called.

Some other friends named their home "Popin"—and the name is part of their address when sending them a letter. They want friends and family and neighbors to know they are always welcome to "pop in" for a cup of tea and a digestive biscuit. (I know it sounds awful, but they really are delicious. Sort of like a dense, round graham cracker and often coated with chocolate.)

Since God is our refuge and dwelling place, maybe some of the things that characterize Him should also characterize our homes as we seek to make them places of refuge for our families.

God is our refuge. Deuteronomy 33:27 says, "The eternal God is your refuge, and underneath are the everlasting arms." I love that! It makes me think of a mother's arms, always open to her children. My mother and I tell my children repeatedly that they are never too big to fit in our arms—no matter how big they grow.

But, like children, we must choose to run to Him. Ruth 2:12 says that it is under God's wings that we take refuge, but we must choose to come for that refuge. Arms are open, wings are ready—what will you choose?

And He is our dwelling place, as well. But we must choose to move in.

Refuge and *dwelling*—two words that make me think of home. Our homes are our dwellings. And our homes should be a refuge for our families. So what does that look like?

A refuge is a place of safety, a place to escape danger. In a refuge, we find shelter and peace and comfort.

In Ephesians 6:12, the apostle Paul points out that we live in the midst of a battle:

> For our struggle is not against flesh and blood, but against the rulers, against the authorities, against the powers of this dark world and against the spiritual forces of evil in the heavenly realms.

The spiritual world is at war, and the physical world is often at war as well. The world can be a dangerous place for our families, and they need a place of refuge—a place of safety and protection.

The world presses in to influence our children. Friends tell them what's right, what's cool. Work pressures pile on our husbands, and they face temptations to relieve the pressure through gambling or pornography or alcohol or, well, you fill in the blank.

I want Toben to long for our home, to feel like Anne's husband, Gilbert, who said, "When a fellow has a home and a dear, little, red-haired wife in it, what more need he ask of life?"[13]

It would be wonderful if our homes offered the kind of refuge our families long for—the place they run to in times of trouble or stress or fatigue. Our homes should be the safest place our families can imagine. When trouble looms, getting home should be the first thought they have.

How can we make our homes a refuge for our families?

In L. M. Montgomery's book *Emily Climbs,* young Emily Starr realizes that "houses are like people—some you like and some you don't like—and once in a while there is one you love."[14] Those are the houses that have become homes.

My sister's favorite book as a child was *The Best Nest* by P. D. Eastman. In it, Mr. Bird sings, "I love my house, I love my nest. In all the world, my nest is best." But Mrs. Bird doesn't like their little home, and so they set off to find what she deems the perfect home. They try one place and then another, only to return at the end of the book to their same old bird house. When it's filled with a new little family, she too sings, "I love my house, I love my nest. In all the world, this nest is best!"

So what makes a house a home? What takes an empty structure and turns it into the kind of home we long for? A place where we—and others—feel welcome and safe?

It's not perfection—let's get that out of the way up front. Perfection can be cold and impersonal—a perfect house can end up feeling more like a museum than a home. Who wants to live in a place where you feel like you have to be quiet and never touch anything? No, thank you!

As Mrs. Bird discovered, a family makes a house a home. A home must be lived in—filled with laughter, and cherished memories. "You have to live in a house before it's home. Not just be happy in it, but work in it, suffer in it, build up memories."[15]

Houses without people are just houses. I love to walk through model homes in new developments (taking along my camera to snap photos of particularly good decorating ideas!). I love seeing how rooms are painted, furniture is arranged, and knickknacks are placed. The models that feel most homey are those with pictures on the walls, toys and clothes in the closets, and dishes on the tables. It seems almost as if the family who lives there just stepped outside for a moment and will be back in just a minute. It should come as no surprise that furnished houses sell faster than empty ones.

Home is more than just a place to sleep at night. To make a house into a home, we must spend time in it, live in it, create memories and traditions in it. We must fill a house with laughter and tears to somehow transform it into a home.

God makes a house into a home. Walk through your house and invite Him in. At the front door, pray that people would feel welcome as they enter your house, that they would notice a difference between your home and an ordinary house.

In the kitchen and where you eat dinner, pray that God would sustain your family with healthy food and that He would sit at the table with you.

Where you sit and play, pray that God would be present in conversation, that He would fill your home with laughter and joy.

In your children's rooms, pray that God would watch over them as they sleep. That their dreams would be filled with visions of Him.

In your bedroom, pray for your marriage.

You can even pray in the bathrooms—that beauty in your family would come from within. That the light of God would shine in their faces and people would recognize it.

A Home Filled with God's Character

According to Job 25:2, God is a God of order. "[H]e establishes order in the heights of heaven." Paul writes, "For God is not a God of disorder but of peace" (1 Corinthians 14:33).

Order helps create a home. It offers a place for things, a routine of life, a system to manage everything.

Have you ever been in a house that's filled with disorder? Or do *you*, perhaps, live in a disordered house? Having small children at home can make this a tough issue. Kids make messes—that's a fact, plain and simple. There are times I've walked into the playroom and been certain a tornado blew through while I was in the kitchen making dinner.

As mothers, we can pick up the tornado ourselves, or we can teach our children the value of order by helping them learn to take care of their things. (This is much easier to do when we learn the lesson ourselves first!) For Audrey and Emma, that means putting away one thing before playing with the next. They are welcome to create huge messes—building forts and making houses for their dolls to play in—and they do. But when they are done playing, they must learn to clean it up.

Order. A place for everything and everything in its place, as the saying goes. Order helps make home a refuge for our families because order is safe. Predictable. Within the boundaries of order we find freedom to live and work.

Order—not perfection. Who wants to live in a perfect house? Not me! Have you ever been in a house that was too perfect? So perfect you felt uncomfortable? Perfection like that can feel stifling as we talk in hushed tones, afraid to leave a footprint in the perfectly vacuumed carpet, afraid to move for fear we'll break something priceless.

Where perfection is rigid, order is flexible.

When Audrey was in the middle of working on a Presidents' Day poster for school, the dining room table was covered with papers, books, poster board, notes on Abraham Lincoln, markers, pencils, and glue for days on end. Rome was not built in a day, and school projects are rarely completed in a day either— especially in the second grade.

During their most recent weeklong vacation from school, Audrey, Emma, and I sewed clothes for their American Girl dolls. Out came the sewing machine, piles of fabric, bits of rickrack and other trim, scissors, and thread. We sewed from time to time over the course of the week, and the order in our home adjusted to the temporary disorder.

Order flexes to the needs of our family.

What's the order to your home, the rhythm to your week?

What time do you get up and go to bed? When do you eat dinner? Is there a time for doing homework, a time to play and have fun?

Order can help create peace. I read this passage recently and want it to be true of my home:

> There was a sense of harmony in the house. The things in it did not have to become acquainted but were good friends from the very start. They did not shriek at each other. There was not a noisy room in the house.[16]

☙

God is also a God of peace. He is called *Yawhew Shalom*, "The LORD Is Peace."

Peace is established when we all get along, when we work together, when we use our inside voices.

Is your home peaceful? Is it harmonious?

Are disagreements dealt with quickly, or do we let feelings of anger and hostility simmer under the surface unchecked? Do we speak to each other kindly, or do we use harsh words and a sarcastic tone?

To let peace rule our homes, we must develop peace within ourselves.

> Let the peace of Christ rule in your hearts, since as members of one body you were called to peace. (Colossians 3:15)

God is a God of beauty. Just take a look around—God's work is breathtaking! Oceans, lakes, rivers, mountains, valleys, and plains. No matter where we live, God's beauty surrounds us.

God's own dwelling place was designed with beauty in mind. From the tabernacle to the temple, in the Old Testament we see beauty's importance in God's dwelling. God didn't choose just anyone to build and decorate His house. In Exodus, we see that God gave special skill and ability to those He chose. Listen to what Moses told the people in Exodus 35:30–35:

> See, the LORD has chosen Bezalel...and he has filled him with the Spirit of God, with skill, ability and knowledge in all kinds of crafts.... And he has given both him and Oholiab...the ability to teach others. He has filled them with skill to do all kinds of work as craftsmen, designers, embroiderers in blue, purple and scarlet yarn and fine linen, and weavers—all of them master craftsmen and designers.

God values beauty, and we are made in His image. (Just think—all those hours spent watching HGTV can be used to reflect God's image!)

I don't know about you, but it's exciting to me that God values our desire to create beauty. How freeing to realize that we shouldn't feel bad or guilty for wanting to live in a beautiful home. I encourage you to stop right now and ask Him to fill you with "skill, ability and knowledge in all kinds of crafts" and "the ability to teach others."

My daily prayer book translates Psalm 65:4 this way: "Happy are they whom you have chosen and drawn into Your courts. They will be satisfied by the beauty and holiness of Your house." Scribbled at the bottom of the page are these words:

God's house is a good place to be! Does my home reflect God's house? Are people satisfied by the beauty and holiness found within its walls?

I want visitors to find rest and peace and beauty when they enter my house. One of the greatest compliments I've received is when people say they feel at home in my home.

Don't you love to be invited into someone's beautiful home and just sit and be satisfied with the beauty of it? I love to sink into a comfortable couch or chair and soak in the atmosphere around me. Colors soothe, objects tell stories, and love is in the air.

How do we create beauty in our homes?

Eliminate clutter. That's the first thing that comes to my mind. It's hard to relax in a room cluttered with stuff. Practice putting things away and teach your husband and your children to do the same.

"But my husband is messy—I've tried," you say. Well, persevere. And if he still doesn't get it, do it for him. It may not seem fair, but it's worth doing yourself when the result is creating a space in which he can rest and relax.

Use color. God created so many colors, each with varying shades and hues. Pick a color scheme for your house and go with it. Just adding a splash of the same color—red, in my case—to every room in your house will tie your home together and give it a sense of visual unity. Paint isn't expensive, and if you don't like it you can always repaint it a different color. Pick colors you love, colors you look good in, colors that soothe.

Add something living—plants, flowers, fish. (Tip: If you can't keep houseplants alive, get artificial ones that look real.)

Bring God's creation indoors—seashells, smooth rocks, pinecones. Teach your children to see God's creative design in the things He has made.

Play beautiful music. Turn off the television and let music set the tone for your home—something upbeat when you have to clean, something soothing when you need to rest. Feel free to sing along (although this is something that only you and God may find beautiful). When I sing at the top of my lungs, it's a joyful noise, indeed.

Light candles. I recently returned home from a weekend in Seattle determined to light more candles. The girlfriend I traveled with makes it a habit of coming home from work every night and lighting candles all over her house—just for herself. "It's the romantic single life," she says.

There's no denying that candles add an air of romance and beauty. Everything—and everyone—looks better by candlelight! The flickering light helps me slow down, unwind, move more slowly, and appreciate beauty. Chances are we could all use a little more romance in our lives.

Building Your House

Proverbs 14:1 tells us that a "wise woman builds her house." (Now, I love Home Depot as much as the next person, but somehow I don't think that's what the writer of Proverbs was talking about.)

So how do we build our house? What kind of wisdom does it take?

We need to think about ways in which we can make our home a place of refuge and safety for our families, a place to rest, relax, and escape the pressures of the world. We must move beyond doing the dishes and folding the laundry to creating a space in which our families are nourished spiritually and our children are brought up in the Lord.

Despite my love of being home and my admission to being a homebody, spending a full day at home is a rarity for me. There are groceries to be bought, errands to be run, kids to take to and from school. There's Bible study on Thursday mornings and ballet class on Tuesdays and Fridays.

I wonder if one of the reasons people are so rarely home is that home life has become overwhelming. Our houses are filled to overflowing with stuff we don't want or need and projects half done. The thought of sorting through it all can fill us with dread.

When I think about home, I think about refuge, rest, and safety. A place to be a family. Sure, we're a family no matter where we are, but home is the backdrop for the action. It's where we can let our guard down completely, where we are most often all together, where we create the traditions and memories that define us.

♁

We decided to have a house built when Audrey was a toddler. It was fascinating to watch the structure slowly take shape from the piles of supplies stacked here, there, and everywhere around our lot. We had great fun walking through it each week and seeing the progress made. To watch walls and rooms begin to take shape and identify them: "That's Audrey's room with the window seat," or "Look! There's our closet!"

> Unless the Lord builds the house, its builders labor in vain.
>
> PSALM 127:1

I think there are some fun parallels between building an actual house and building our homes, like Proverbs 14:1 talks about. For example, it takes wisdom to build a house—whether an actual structure with four walls and a roof or the homes we create within those walls.

Before the first shovel of dirt was dug on our empty lot, we realized that building a house would require an investment—a hefty investment. We saved and saved, gladly giving up some things so we could afford the house we wanted. Somehow a day on the ski slopes, a fancy meal out, or a week's vacation didn't seem as important as the house. With our new house in mind, our priorities changed.

We learned to operate on a new schedule when we were told up front that it would take time to build our house. After walking through the model, we were ready to move in immediately. But building a house doesn't happen overnight. It took time.

We chose our floor plan. Which one did we want? There were a bunch of different houses to choose from, and we spent time thinking about the one that we liked best, the one that would suit our family.

After all those decisions were made, the builder took measurements, placed stakes, dug a giant hole, and poured a foundation. The weather had to be just right and the foundation had to be sound before anything could be built upon it. More time! If the foundation isn't solid and set, the builder won't build. He knows that rushing ahead will just mean tearing it down and starting again later.

⌒

Sometimes giving up things—saying no to things that we like, we think are fun, and we want—means we gain much more in the long run. We must make wise choices about the things on which we spend our time, money, energy, and emotions.

As we "build our houses"—the houses Moses describes— we must realize that it requires an investment. Creating a home that provides rest and refuge and safety for our families takes time and energy. It takes hard work! But viewing those trying days when we fall into bed exhausted as an investment in our families makes it easier to get up and do it again tomorrow. It makes it easier to say no to some things when we realize we're choosing something better and more valuable in the long run.

Because as we "build our houses" our priorities change—sometimes by choice, sometimes by necessity. Putting family first began with marriage—putting my husband first—and continued with the birth of our first child.

With marriage, I began to learn to put Toben's needs and wants ahead of my own as I struggled to understand what putting others ahead of myself looks like in real life.

> Do nothing out of selfish ambition or vain conceit, but in humility consider others better than yourselves. Each of you should look not only to your own interests, but also to the interests of others.
>
> PHILIPPIANS 2:3-4

With Audrey's birth, my priority for sleep (ordinarily pretty high!) moved lower down the list when compared with a crying baby. I gladly gave up sleep to attend to her needs. She became my greatest priority. Even today, doing lunch duty at school is far from my favorite thing, but because Audrey has asked me to do it, I do. It's more important to me that she knows I care about her than for me to go with my desire and not do it at all.

In our instant society, it's hard to wait for things. We want what we want and we want it now. But building a house takes time—time to plan, time to build, time to grow and develop as we learn what works and what doesn't.

It's so easy for me to get discouraged because our home isn't exactly the way I dream of it being. I often fall into the trap of looking only at the end goal instead of enjoying and learning from the process. I forget that things take time. It takes time to make a home, as Leslie Ford said to Anne Blythe in *Anne's House of Dreams*: "Now, it's just a house to you—but the years will make it a home."

It helps me to remember that my house won't look exactly like yours. There are all different kinds of families—big families and small families, busy families and not-so-busy families. As we build our houses, we get to choose what we want it to look like. And if we don't like something, we can change it.

Have you ever felt overwhelmed by your schedule and amazed at all that life has become? I sure have. I often stop and remind myself of all the choices I've made that have put me where I am. Saying yes instead of no is the one that comes most readily to mind. We make so many choices each day—often without thinking. To build our houses wisely, we must choose wisely—in the big and the small things.

Building on the Rock

The foundation on which we build our houses is so important. Remember the song about the wise man and the foolish man?

> The wise man built his house upon the rock,
> The wise man built his house upon the rock,
> The wise man built his house upon the rock,
> And the rains came a-tumblin' down!
> The rains came down and the floods came up,
> The rains came down and the floods came up,
> The rains came down and the floods came up,
> And the house on the rock stood firm.

We can choose to build our house wisely (on the rock) or foolishly (on the sand). When all is bright and sunny, both surfaces may appear sound. In fact, in sunny weather the sandy spot is often preferable—who wouldn't want to live right on the beach with the ocean at your back door?

But then the storm comes and knocks one flat.

I love how this story is told in the Gospel of Luke. Jesus said,

> "I will show you what he is like who comes to me and hears my words and puts them into practice. He is like a man building a house, who dug down deep and laid the foundation on rock. When a flood came, the torrent struck that house but could not shake it, because it was well built. But the one who hears my words and does not put them into practice is like a man who built a house on the ground without a foundation. The moment the torrent struck that house, it collapsed and its destruction was complete." (Luke 6:47–49)

I think building your house without a foundation looks like copying someone else. For example, we see another family and pattern ourselves after them, rather than doing what's best for our own families. We're so good at comparing ourselves with others, aren't we?

The world has a lot to say about what our lives should be like, and the messages are often conflicting. Trying to keep up will leave us running around rebuilding—a little like changing our minds throughout the building process, tearing down walls and putting up new ones and never getting the house built.

What does it look like to build your house on the rock? Building my house on the rock means digging down deep to lay the foundation on the rock. It means seeking God's wisdom in each and every decision I make concerning my family. It means constantly evaluating our family and making sure the decisions we've made honor Him and are still working. It means recognizing those times when I'm tempted to make a decision to fit in with everyone around me, rather than making a decision based on what God has taught me.

Ultimately, building my house on the rock means building my house on the Rock. It means working on my relationship with God, pursuing Him. Spending time with Him in prayer and in His Word. It means getting well enough acquainted with God—His character and His attributes—to make wise decisions confidently...because I *know* Him.

So often we wonder if what we're doing is what God wants us to do. Digging down deep and pursuing our relationship with God is one of the primary ways God reveals Himself to us.

Think about your husband for a minute. You already know whether he'll like something or not, or what he will think about a decision you make...because you *know* him. You've spent time with him, you've talked with him, you've dug down deep in your relationship. You have the confidence to say to a friend, "He'd love that!" when she invites you to dinner. Or to say, "He'd hate that!" when she invites your family to go camping. (Toben hates camping—after giving it a good shot two summers ago. And I have to admit that almost a week of camping without a shower was too much for me, too!)

God is *Yahweh Tsuri*, the LORD My Rock. Here's what I learned about this name of God from *Praying the Names of God* by Ann Spangler:

> Rocks provided shade, shelter, and safety in the wilderness and were used to construct altars, temples, houses, and city walls.... The word "rock" epitomizes his enduring faithfulness.

When tragedy comes, as it inevitably will, and when the world around us begins to tremble and shake, as it inevitably will, we will not be shaken. Instead, the Lord who is the Rock eternal will be there, giving us rest and peace.[17]

Knowing God as my Rock, building my life and my faith upon Him, gives me a sense of security and safety. Worry loses its hold on my life because my home is built on a sure foundation—one that cannot be shaken. When we build our homes upon the Rock, they reflect Him—solid, unchanging, eternal, steadfast, steady, secure, and sure.

Use Your Power Wisely

Proverbs 14:1 goes on to say, "With her own hands the foolish one tears hers down."

It's a little overwhelming sometimes to think of the great power we wield as women. We have the ability to build a house and the ability to tear it down—often in a remarkably short amount of time. Pursuing wisdom is so important. We must seek God and His guidance each moment and be intentional about the choices we make for our homes and families.

Another fascinating Bible study I've done is *Five Aspects of Woman* by Barbara Mouser. In it she describes five different roles we play as women: Mistress of the Domain, Helper-Completer, Lifegiver, Lady of Wisdom, and Glory of Man. You can find more information about these roles and this study at fiveaspects.org.

As homemakers, I think one of the primary ways we build our homes is by setting the tone for our families. The saying "If Mama ain't happy, ain't nobody happy" is trite but true. Our attitudes and examples have a huge effect on our families.

In a Jewish family, it is the woman who lights the candles to bring in the Sabbath. In much the same way, it is the woman who brings light into the home—more than any other member of the family. She creates an atmosphere in which her husband and children can live and prosper; she is the core of the family unit.

The tone, the feel, the look...all are because of her influence. When a wife is happy and positive, even the most depressed husband or tired child will absorb her energy and be uplifted. Conversely, if she is unhappy and the home has a feeling of negativity, it too will affect the whole family. [18]

I see this so often in the mornings. If I'm stressed out—getting the girls ready for school in a rush, serving breakfast in a hurry, and tearing through my closet like a madwoman—my craziness rubs off on them. I've also noticed that when we are rushed in the mornings, it's nearly impossible for Audrey and Emma to have a good day at school, or church, or wherever we go. Audrey cries at the bus stop, Emma whines for most of the day, and I find myself wishing we could all go back to bed and start over.

Because of this, I try to plan our mornings carefully by getting everyone up a little earlier, sitting down to eat breakfast as a family, and making time to read together. In this way, I can send each one off to face her day in the best possible space.

I have great memories of breakfast time as a child. During my fifth grade year, my dad was stationed at Maxwell Air Force Base in Montgomery, Alabama. Our kitchen had a bay window with a table tucked in the nook. Mom always set the table for breakfast—bowls and spoons laid out properly, orange juice in a pitcher—and we began our day together as a family. We held hands as we prayed, and we finished the meal with a devotion or story. I remember mornings in general as being leisurely, calm, and relaxed. (Of course, my mother may remember otherwise. But somehow I think crazy, rushed mornings were rare, since the aura of peace and calm is what remains in my memory.)

To do this for my own family, I've found that my day has to start off right before anyone else is up. I'm a morning person, so this isn't too difficult for me. Early morning is when I dig down deep in my relationship with God. I love being awake before anyone else and having the house all to myself. I make coffee, feed the cat, let the dog out, and light candles. The kitchen table is where God and I meet each morning.

I read my Bible while I drink my coffee, pen in hand to mark anything that stands out. I'm currently reading through the Gospels. While I read the stories of Jesus, I'm reminded of hearing them as a child and am overwhelmed once again by the wonder of His miracles, the compassion He showed to people, and the aching loneliness He must have felt on the cross.

After reading, I pray for Toben and Audrey and Emma. I've taken my copies of *The Power of a Praying Wife* and *The Power of a Praying Parent* by Stormie O'Martian and had them spiral-bound. I flip through a chapter each day, and in this way it takes me about a month to get through each book. I pray through these books over and over, adding my own specific requests and recording them in the margins. I love looking back on what I prayed for and seeing how God answered each request.

Praying for my family—for daily things, like safety on the school bus and in traffic; and for bigger requests, like health and friendships—helps free me from worry. I place my family and my concerns into God's hands, trusting that He will hold it all safe.

My time with God each day lasts anywhere from thirty minutes to an hour. If you've never done this, that may sound like a lot. But you'll be amazed at how the time flies. For me, taking this time in the morning assures me that no matter what the day brings, it has started well.

Just last Saturday I missed my morning time with God. I rationalized that I'd fit it in later, since both days over the weekend were wide open. But something felt "off" the rest of the day. I was grumpy and dissatisfied. I couldn't put my finger on exactly what it was that had me out of sorts. I tried to shake it, but the underlying foul mood wouldn't leave.

After two days of this, I began fresh on Monday morning with God. My day felt lighter, I felt happier, the dissatisfaction was gone.

Coincidence? Perhaps. But real or not, time with God first thing in the morning works for me.

Of course, God wants us to walk with Him throughout each moment of the day. And ending the day with Him is important, too. But there's something to be said for making this time in the morning rather than at night. The psalms in particular have a lot to say about time spent with God in the morning:

In the morning, O LORD, you hear my voice;
in the morning I lay my requests before you
and wait in expectation. (Psalm 5:3)

But I cry to you for help, O LORD;
in the morning my prayer comes before you.
(Psalm 88:13)

Let the morning bring me word of your unfailing love,
for I have put my trust in you.
Show me the way I should go,
for to you I lift up my soul. (Psalm 143:8)

Jesus, too, spent time with His Father early in the morning. "Very early in the morning, while it was still dark, Jesus got up, left the house and went off to a solitary place, where he prayed" (Mark 1:35).

Why the morning? Because much like houses and homes, we build our days from the ground up, and a good foundation is important.

It's a wonderful feeling to face my day having talked with God about all that's on my calendar. I love to pray about each item and ask God to give me the strength and energy—*His* strength and *His* energy—to move through my day with grace and love and patience.

Who couldn't use more of that?

It's so much harder to start down a grumpy path and have to switch directions at noon than to start well first thing. I can't encourage you enough to try it—you'll see a difference, I promise!

Don't expect it to just happen, though. Start by setting your alarm for an earlier wake-up—perhaps just fifteen minutes before your usual time. Fill the coffeepot the night before. Decide where you'll spend your time; then set out your Bible, a notebook, and a pen.

And if it doesn't happen the first time, try again. Keep at it until you find a rhythm and routine that works for you.

If you've not spent much time reading through your Bible and aren't sure where to start, I suggest the book of Psalms. Most of the chapters are short and express such real and honest emotions—emotions that will reflect your own. Many can be used as prayers. They are a wonderful example of being completely real and honest with God.

Another great place to begin is the book of Philippians. It can easily be read in a sitting or two. And no matter how many times I read it, I always discover something new—a verse that stands out to me in a different light, an encouragement I hadn't noticed before.

One Thing In, One Thing Out

As I said earlier, when we moved to Southern California we got rid of everything we didn't absolutely love. The result is that about 90 percent of what's left is associated with stories, emotions, and memories.

While I'm not going to go overboard and say I love cleaning house (who loves scrubbing toilets?), I will tell you that it is a much easier task when my house contains things I care about.

Moving into a smaller house was more of a necessity than a choice when we moved to San Diego. But having lived in a smaller house for three years now, I can honestly say I prefer it. As I dream about the future, I realize that I *hope* we stay in a smaller house.

We're conditioned by society to pursue bigger and better with each change. But more isn't always better; sometimes more is just more. So how do we choose less when it comes to our homes?

When my aunt and uncle moved to Southern California they downsized in a big way. They moved from a large house to a one-bedroom mobile home—600 or so square feet—located just half a block from the beach. They planned on it being temporary, a place to spend holiday weekends when they bought their "real" house. That was more than six years ago!

For them, living in such a small space means living with less—there's no way to fudge. As a result, they carefully consider every purchase. Bringing in something new means something else must go out.

I like that idea. We donate a lot of used items, especially toys. Knowing their toys are going to children who don't have as much makes it easier for my children to give up their worn-out or outgrown things, particularly those items they loved in the past.

I remember reading a story in which the main character only

owned a certain number of items at all times. She kept the number consistent—one new thing in, one old thing out.

I can't imagine counting every single thing in my house, but I understand the appeal of this idea.

Choosing less in a house has its advantages. For example, I can clean my entire house really well in about an hour or two, and I can vacuum every room without switching outlets.

A smaller house also holds less stuff, making it necessary to say no to many things we just don't need. And of course, a smaller house costs less than a bigger one!

God's Home on Earth

God knows the importance of having a place to call home.

It's fascinating to me to think that even God has a house. "He stretches out the heavens like a canopy, and spreads them out like a tent to live in" (Isaiah 40:22).

Despite making His home in the heavens, God wanted a house on earth too. After leaving captivity in Egypt, the Israelites headed into the desert, where God said, "Have them make a sanctuary for me, and I will dwell among them" (Exodus 25:8).

Doesn't that seem extraordinary? That God, who created the whole universe and rides on the wind, as the psalmist says (Psalm 104:3), would come to live on earth in a tent?

The tabernacle, as God's house was called in Exodus, was indeed God's home—the place where He dwelt. While most of us don't live in a tent, our homes today and God's tabernacle home are similar in several ways.

First of all, God's home reflected His character—it was designed in a particular way and contained many beautiful things. And each of those things had a purpose and a story. From the entrance facing east toward the rising sun to the curtain separating the holy place from the Holy of Holies, God's tabernacle home was filled with beautiful items of remarkable craftsmanship. Colors and textures abounded.

> If you'd like to learn more about the tabernacle and how each part of it was fulfilled in Christ Jesus, I highly recommend *A Woman's Heart: God's Dwelling Place* by Beth Moore. This was the first Beth Moore Bible study I did, and now I'm hooked!

After God's people settled in Israel, King Solomon built a new home for God. Unlike the movable tabernacle, the temple was a permanent structure—larger and more elaborate. But just like the tabernacle, God's temple in Jerusalem was built according to specific instructions. And once again, the things that filled this new house each had meaning and purpose. In fact, some of the items in God's new house were old things from the tabernacle.

When dedicating the temple, Solomon said, "But will God really dwell on earth? The heavens, even the highest heaven, cannot contain you. How much less this temple I have built!" (1 Kings 8:27).

Wouldn't it be wonderful if the things in our homes had similar meaning? Perhaps it's time to come up with new criteria as we sort through closets and attics, basements and boxes. Don't panic—not everything has to have a specific purpose to get a spot in the "keep" pile. While objects in the tabernacle did serve a purpose, they were also beautiful.

For some things, their function or purpose is just to be beautiful and bring a smile to your face when you see it. You only have to look in a garden, at a sunset, or the faces of your children to know that God places high value on beauty. So the teacup collection can stay, even if it only gets used from time to time; the same goes for your apron collection.

Today, we often refer to our church building as God's house—just think how many houses God has around the world! But *we* ourselves are also God's home. Listen to Jesus' words to His disciples in John 14:23–24:

> "If anyone loves me, he will obey my teaching. My Father will love him, and *we will come to him and make our home with him.*"

Wow! (That verse has a huge exclamation point next to it in my Bible.)

Paul writes to the church in Corinth, "Don't you know that you yourselves are God's temple and that God's Spirit lives in you?" (1 Corinthians 3:16). He goes on to say, "God's temple is sacred, and *you are that temple*" (3:17). In another letter to the same church, he writes, "For we are the temple of the living God" (2 Corinthians 6:16).

How exciting! When we accept God's offer of salvation, "Christ will live in you as you open the door and invite him in" (Ephesians 3:17, *The Message*). It gives the idea of *home* whole new meaning, doesn't it? To think that God makes His home within each of us—warts and all—is amazing to me.

And just like we do, God takes great interest in His home. He maintains and cares for it, He furnishes it with the things that He loves and values, and from time to time He rearranges things completely.

A home requires care—from the chores that are done every day to bigger projects done from time to time. There's daily cleaning and spring cleaning. Painting an entire room, and doing a quick touch-up when you move a picture and leave a hole in the wall.

I like the truth in this quote from *The Grass Harp*: "If you sweep a house, and tend its fires and fill its stove, and there is love in you all the years you are doing this, then you and that house are married, that house is yours."[19]

God cares for each of us in the same way. We need food and clothes, which Jesus assures us God will provide:

"Therefore I tell you, do not worry about your life, what you will eat or drink; or about your body, what you will wear.... Look at the birds.... Are you not more valuable than they?" (Matthew 6:25–26)

When we first moved into our house, there was a lot of work to be done: carpets needed to be replaced, light fixtures to be bought and installed, cabinets painted. Plus, the whole house needed a good cleaning from top to bottom. (Luckily it's a smaller house, so it didn't take too long!)

When we invite God to live in us, there is similar work to be done: habits needing a change, attitudes to have light shed on, thought lives that could use a thorough going-over. As seasons in our lives change, we sort through these things—a spring cleaning of the soul, if you will. We once again evaluate our thoughts and attitudes, sweep hidden places clean, and shine light into the corners.

In both spiritual and daily home care, life has its mundane tasks. There are meals to cook, dishes to wash, plants to water. Ironing and mending, dusting and polishing.

As the old saying goes:

Wash on Monday,
Iron on Tuesday,
Mend on Wednesday,
Churn on Thursday,
Clean on Friday,
Bake on Saturday,
Rest on Sunday.[20]

I think one of the best things about having a home is getting to fill it with treasures—but not too many! Besides my family, I love filling my home with beautiful things. It's so much fun to find that wonderful item—especially when it's an antique—and to know just where it will go in the house.

We must take care, when furnishing our homes, to fill them with objects that are useful, beautiful, uplifting, and beneficial to our families.

God furnishes His home in us as well. As we invite Him to make Himself at home, He brings with him those things He finds useful and beautiful—those things that make Him feel at home in our hearts. Things like love, joy, peace, patience, kindness, goodness, faithfulness, gentleness, and self-control—the fruit of His Spirit.

Isn't it wonderful that God brings such things with Him when He moves into our lives? He takes the shell of our lives and turns it into a home for Himself—and for us, too, by filling it with beautiful treasures.

My mother loves to rearrange her furniture. I can remember coming home from elementary school to find my mother and her best friend collapsed on the floor laughing, worn out from lugging couches, tables, and chairs all over the house. Sometimes my bedroom wasn't even where I had left it that morning—my mother had switched it with my sister's! Dad would come home and shake his head with a smile. He understood that sometimes you just need a change.

God, too, rearranges His home from time to time. He allows circumstances to change rapidly, making patience the focal point of our lives. He adds a baby to the family, and joy moves to the forefront. Trials come, and faithfulness gets more wear than it did before.

The difference is that God never moves on. Once He takes up residence within our souls, *He will never leave.* "I will never leave you or forsake you," He tells us again and again (Deuteronomy 31:6, 8; Joshua 1:5; 1 Kings 8:57; Hebrews 13:5). No home is beyond His repair, no home improvement project too big or expensive or messy or time-consuming to undertake. He may knock down walls, and it may be painful, but the home He is building in our lives is beyond what any of us could imagine as our dream house.

The Home I'm Longing For

While we provide a home for God here on earth, God is building another home for us. Our bodies here on earth need shelter, but our souls were created for the eternal home of heaven.

God entrusted this building project to Jesus, who told His disciples,

> "In my Father's house are many rooms; if it were not so, I would have told you. I am going there to prepare a place for you. And if I go and prepare a place for you, I will come back and take you to be with me that you also may be where I am." (John 14:2–3)

Do you long for home?

It would be wonderful if our homes were places our husbands and children longed for. If the place we call home created a yearning in their hearts for eternity.

Jesus wants us to *desire* coming home to be with Him.

"Come home, come home.
Ye who are weary, come home."

Softly and tenderly, Jesus is calling,
Calling, "O Sinner, come home."[21]

Heaven. While I've used this word before to describe things like a day at the spa, the view at the beach in Carmel, wandering through a bookstore alone, or a particularly chocolate-y dessert, heaven is really beyond our wildest dreams. But unlike many of our imaginings, heaven is a real place with real people and a spot reserved just for me—and you!

Can you even begin to imagine it? Jesus is calling us to come home to heaven—our real home, the place for which we were created. It thrills my heart to think that heaven is everything I hope and dream a home should be. To take all those thoughts and feelings about home that can hardly be put into words and know that in heaven they will be filled beyond "anything I can ask or imagine," as Paul writes (Ephesians 3:20).

In heaven we will really and truly be home. In that home God has prepared for us, we will find peace and rest, safety and joy, family and love—forever.

As a child, I imagined heaven to be rather dull. Sure, it *sounded* beautiful...but a little boring, too.

My earthly home was also something I took for granted—I didn't know much about the world, and my home seemed rather ordinary. However, as I've grown and seen more and more of the world and its offerings, I've come to cherish home as something to be treasured and appreciated, guarded and protected.

Heaven, too, has become more sacred to me. No longer dull, heaven is a place I dream of and hope for with a longing I can't quite describe. Life seems more and more like a journey, and heaven the home I'm heading for—no matter how wonderful the sights along the way.

I love home because sometimes it looks a little bit like heaven. I am intrigued by this perspective offered by the Unicorn at the end of *The Last Battle*, the final book in the Chronicles of

Narnia. Upon entering true Narnia, the life after life in the Old Narnia, he says:

> I have come home at last! This is my real country! I belong here. This is the land I have been looking for all my life, though I never knew it till now. The reason why we loved the old Narnia is that it sometimes looked a little like this.[22]

"I wouldn't give up my family for anything—
not for all the chocolate in the world."

CHARLIE, IN *CHARLIE AND THE CHOCOLATE FACTORY*

A Simple Family

AS A CHILD, MY FAMILY WAS MY WORLD. FAMILY represented everything that was safe, sure, and unchanging in my world. It was my anchor—the one thing holding me close and safe in a world that seemed big and unknowable.

Because my dad was in the Air Force, we moved with predictable frequency. From California to Colorado. From Colorado to Alabama. From Alabama to England. From England back to the States. New schools, new churches, new houses, new faces, and new friends were the stuff of growing up for me.

The only thing that remained the same was my family. It didn't matter where we were in the world; as long as Mom, Dad, Kristen, and I were together, we were home.

In all my growing up years, we never lived near other family. We visited them and they visited us, but the bulk of holidays and Sunday dinners were spent as a family of four. I do have a few memories of an Easter or Christmas spent with grandparents and cousins, aunts and uncles. But for the most part, the word *family* meant just the four of us.

We moved to England when I was eleven. It was the longest flight I'd ever taken, and I spent it trying to sleep while half sitting up, half leaning on my mother's lap. I remember emerging from the airport into the hustle and bustle of a noisy London morning. Cars whizzing by on the wrong side of the road, people loudly speaking English in a way I'd never before heard—the words familiar, yet foreign.

By the time we settled in at the bed and breakfast that evening, I was tired, lonely, and scared. Change was something familiar to me, but this time it felt different. It was like we'd landed on another planet. I was desperate to return to the world I knew.

Have you ever experienced jet lag? If so, you know how I felt as I lay there in that strange bed, exhausted and unable to sleep. My worries grew as they raced through my head. The sounds of the street outside grated on my nerves, and I wanted to cry. I remember staring at the ceiling and then looking around the room, knowing my family was there. Quite suddenly, I knew it would be okay. Because we were together.

Building a Strong Family

Looking back, I am so thankful that I grew up in the family I did. Sure, Kristen and I argued and fought (little sisters can't help but be annoying at times!), I disagreed with my parents, and we all needed an occasional break from each other. That's normal. But my family loved each other—and I'm grateful for that. My family is the model for me as Toben and I create our own family.

Madeline L'Engle was once asked about the best thing she and her husband ever did for their children. She said:

I answered immediately and without thinking, "We love each other."[23]

I love this response because I know my parents would say the same thing.

Perhaps you grew up in a family like mine. But maybe you didn't, and the word *family* is something that conjures painful memories instead of happy ones. As speaker and author Beth Moore writes, "We don't have to come from particularly healthy families to place a high premium on family relationships."[24]

The good news is that just as we build our house, so we also build our families. We can choose to build a family that is strong, loving, and provides safety and love for each of its members.

So how do we build strong families? How do we create memories, traditions, and joy in our families so that family lasts and is something our children value and cherish? How do we build our families upon God's Word and His principles so our families shine in a world of darkness?

Like our homes, family has become overwhelming for many of us. As mothers, we often feel as if we bear the sole responsibility for our families. We grow weary and burned out from working to keep our families together and strong.

The mother of a friend of mine died a few years ago. As he mourned for her, he realized that he was also grieving for the loss of his family. His mother had been the glue keeping the family intact; there was no longer anything to bring the family together. With her death, he lost not only his mother, but also much of his relationships with his siblings and his father.

Another friend is dealing with the same thing. Her mother died and she too is grieving the loss of her entire family with her mother's passing. She's struggling to reconcile the loss and to understand what her role in the family is now that her mother is no longer there to define and create family for them.

Is it wrong that mothers are so often the glue holding families together? I don't think so. Nevertheless it makes me wonder how heartbroken those mothers would be to see that their families died along with them.

As a mother, I want to build a strong family—but I don't want to be the family all on my own.

As I said earlier, I feel so blessed to grow up with the family I did. To me, my family seemed rather ordinary—a mom and a dad, two daughters, an assortment of dogs, and one cat who won my heart by having kittens in the spare room. My parents loved each other deeply and I don't remember a single instance of them fighting—or even arguing.

Of course, Kristen and I bickered often. As siblings are wont to do, we went through seasons of fiercely loving or hating each other. We played Barbies, we played dress-up, we built forts with blankets and bar stools.

My mother didn't work outside the home, and she was nearly always there when I came home from school. When she wasn't, I felt strangely lost.

The cookie jar was always full of homemade cookies; my lunch was always packed for me; and my mother usually included a note letting me know she would be praying for me during my math quiz, my French vocabulary test, or in whatever challenges I faced that day at school.

Dinner was at 5:30, and we all sat around the table to eat and talk about our days. Dad led our family in devotions after dinner, and when we were young, he or Mom would read aloud from the *Chronicles of Narnia* while the dirty dishes sat waiting in the sink.

We played Rummy 500, Monopoly, and Uno. We went camping, took road trips, and skied in a line down the mountain with Dad in the front and Mom bringing up the rear, singing, "Give me wax for my skis, keep me bobbin' through the trees" at the top of our lungs. "Sing hosanna, sing hosanna, sing hosanna to the King of kings!" we yelled.

As I sit here looking at what I've just written, it looks campy, corny, and so completely wonderful. And I realize that my family wasn't ordinary at all. It was extraordinary—wonderful, fun, warm, safe.

I want our little family to be just like my family was.

That's not to say that life was always a bowl of cherries, or that we didn't struggle. There were times I couldn't wait to leave my family and get out on my own. Times when my parents seemed old-fashioned, stifling, and overly protective. Times when I doubted they understood me or the world around us.

But I never doubted their love. And like Charlie, I wouldn't trade them for all the chocolate in the world.

Learning to Love

Maybe your memories of family are filled with pain and disappointment, hurt and sorrow. If that's the case, I can only say how sorry I am. Above all, our families should love us just for being ourselves. They should make us feel safe, accepted, and respected. Through our families, we should see God's love demonstrated.

I was watching an episode of *Mr. Rogers' Neighborhood* with Emma not long ago, and one of the characters said something I found incredibly wise. While heading out to make his deliveries, Mr. McFeely told Mr. Rogers, "We can't love until someone loves us first."

The first Bible verse I ever memorized was 1 John 4:19: "We

love because he first loved us." I don't know if I fully understood the words when I was a child. In fact, I'm not sure I understand them even now—the very fact that God loves *us* is astounding.

To know we are loved allows us to love back. I've heard it said that one of the greatest theological truths known to man is this one: "Jesus loves me, this I know." God knew what He was doing when He told us we had to become like children to enter His kingdom.

We cannot love until we have first been loved.

Family is where we learn to love.

℘

We just don't see a lot of love between families on television these days. When we do, it makes us sit up and take notice—because it's so unusual.

So many television sitcoms today portray the parents as clueless and out-of-touch with their children and the world, and the children as independent and indulgent of their not-so-intelligent parents. On sitcoms today, parents—not children—learn the lessons. It seems so backward.

At brunch after church one Sunday, we sat with a group of friends and started talking about families portrayed on television shows: What families did we see modeled in ways that we wanted to copy?

The answers were few. *Seventh Heaven,* one person suggested. *Little Bear* and *Franklin,* said another. But those last two are cartoon bears and turtles, so we weren't sure they counted.

After brainstorming for some time, we couldn't come up with a single example of a family on a primetime show that we wanted to emulate. So we headed back in time and the answers came a little easier: *The Cosby Show, Leave It to Beaver, Father Knows Best, The Waltons, Little House on the Prairie.*

Parents were wise, children were obedient, lessons were learned by children and taught at home by parents who loved them unconditionally.

I love the *Little House* episode called "The Richest Man in Walnut Grove." In it Pa's crop fails and they are unable to pay their debt at Oleson's Mercantile—after Pa has promised snooty Mrs. Oleson that it will be paid in full by the end of the week.

The entire Ingalls family pulls together. Mary works full-time sewing clothes for the local dressmaker, and Laura takes over Mary's chores so Mary can keep up with her schoolwork at night. Pa mucks out stalls at the local stables and works any odd job he can find. Ma stretches their food supply with creative meals.

The thing that struck me in this episode is that they all pitch in so cheerfully. They're excited about helping each other. The episode drives home the message that when families work together, cooperation and struggle makes them stronger than before.

When the end of the week comes, the Ingalls count their cash, dress up in their best clothes, and go to town—together—to pay the bill. Mrs. Oleson is rude to them, as expected. She's heard they don't have money to pay their debt. Then she gets a surprise—Pa informs her that they have come to pay off their debt. As they leave the store, Mr. Oleson pulls Pa aside and tells him, "With a family like yours, you may be the richest man in Walnut Grove." Pa just smiles. "I know I am," he says.

We don't live on a farm, and our livelihood does not depend upon our laboring all day long. When reading books like *Farmer Boy* or the *American Girl* stories to Audrey and Emma, I'm always amazed by how long and hard the children worked. Tending smaller children, planting the fields, cooking, cleaning, caring for animals—children back then seemed to work harder than many adults today.

So how do families work together today? How do we create that sense of unity, of working together for a common goal, of needing each member of the family to be whole?

Given how much my children—especially Emma—love to help around the house, I think I need to take more advantage of it. Just this morning, Emma put all the silverware away from the dishwasher and sorted all of the laundry, carefully pulling the legs back out of jeans, turning socks and shirts right side out.

Asking for our children's help with the care of our homes means giving up some control. Laundry folded and put away by a child won't look like it was done by you. A floor mopped by little arms will no doubt have a few grimy corners remaining. Teaching kids to do these kinds of jobs may mean tolerating a load or two of pink underwear and socks. But we *all* learn by making mistakes. (And come on, who doesn't love pink underwear? I do! Plus, pink socks match almost anything my girls own.)

Relinquishing control is difficult. It's often faster and easier to do things ourselves. There's less complaining that way, too. "Why do I have to do *all* the work around here?" is something I hear too often when I ask Audrey to let the dog out, or Emma to let her back in.

Excuse me? Who does all the work around here?

If I do, I suppose the fault is my own.

> We talk about the family we are born with, the family we choose, and the church family. The one thing binding all these together is love.

A Family Is Made Up of Many Parts

In the New Testament, the church of believers is often referred to as a body. Numerous sermons have been preached about our need for one another and the distinct role each believer must play in order for the body of Christ to be healthy and to function as it should.

In much the same way, our family is also a body—just on a smaller scale. As individuals, we each play a role in building the body of the family. Paul writes in 1 Corinthians 12 about each member's worth to the body of Christ; this also applies to our families.

Think for a minute about your family—picture each one of them in your mind. The family unit, though it is made up of many people, and though each is different from the rest, forms one family.

Think about 1 Corinthians 12 in terms of your family. It might look like this with a family spin:

Now the family is not made up of one person but of many. If the brother should say, "Because I am not a grown up, I do not belong to the family," he would not for that reason cease to be part of the family. And if the sister should say, "Because I am not the mother, I do not belong to the body," she would not for that reason cease to be part of the family. If the whole body were a father, where would the sense of nurturing be? If the whole body were a child, where would the sense of protection be? But in fact God has arranged the people in the family, every one of them, just as He wanted them to be.

The child cannot say to the parent, "I don't need you!" And the parent cannot say to the child, "I don't need you!"... But God has combined the members of the family so that there should be no division in the family, but that its members should have equal concern for each other. If one suffers, everyone suffers with it; if one is honored, everyone rejoices with it.

The best advice my mother ever gave me as a mother is that I must do what is best for my *whole family*. Not me, not Toben, not Audrey, not Emma—but what is in the best interest of the *entire* family. Of course, doing this means paying attention to each person in my family—to know and understand their needs, wants, and dreams. Only then can I make decisions about our life together that benefit the whole family.

"Rules for Christian Households"

In my Bible, there's a section in Colossians 3 called "Rules for Christian Households." I love how *The Message* paraphrases it:

> Let the peace of Christ keep you in tune with each other, in step with each other. None of this going off and doing your own thing. And cultivate thankfulness. Let the Word of Christ—the Message—have the run of the house. Give it plenty of room in your lives. Instruct and direct one another using good common sense. And sing, sing your hearts out to God! Let every detail in your lives—words, actions, whatever—be done in the name of the Master, Jesus, thanking God the Father every step of the way.
>
> Wives, understand and support your husbands by submitting to them in ways that honor the Master.
>
> Husbands, go all out in love for your wives. Don't take advantage of them.
>
> Children, do what your parents tell you. This delights the Master no end.

Parents, don't come down too hard on your children or you'll crush their spirits. (Colossians 3:15–21, *The Message*)

How I want a family like the one described in this passage!

I just love God's Word, don't you? The more I read it, the more I'm amazed at how much God loves us, knows the details of our lives, and offers the instruction we need to live life His way.

In this passage from Paul, God gives us the key to a simple family—following His Word:

All Scripture is God-breathed and is useful for teaching, rebuking, correcting and training in righteousness, so that the man of God may be thoroughly equipped for every good work. (2 Timothy 3:16–17)

⌒

"Let the peace of Christ keep you in tune with each other, in step with each other" (Colossians 3:15, *The Message*).

Peace. It's one of those words I just love because it seems so elusive. Peace can be hard to find. It's Jesus who keeps us in tune with each other. How wonderful to know that with His help, we can make peace an everyday occurrence for our families. When we build our house on the Rock, we have the same goals, the same foundation.

What are your family's plans for the day, the weekend, the year? What trips do you want to take together? What places do you want to see?

Dream together as a family! Include your children in the decisions you make and let them see how it's done. When you have a decision to make, ask them what they'd do and how they feel about what is going on.

My children are young, so we solicit their input regarding our weekend plans or what to do when they have a day off from school. But they're not yet ready to help make a decision about moving or changing jobs. You know your children—their ages and their maturity level—and can decide what they're ready for.

Finding the Best for the WHOLE Family

"None of this going off and doing your own thing" (Colossians 3:15, *The Message*).

We're back to that great advice my mother gave me—to do what's best for my whole family. As much as I'd like to go off and do my own thing (like heading to the spa instead of the grocery store, or spending money on clothes rather than tuition, or turning left at the airport instead of the bus stop), as a member of my family I'm required to take the rest of them into account.

And it's not just me. This is a lesson that we all need to learn, a lesson I need to teach my children about what it means to be a family. It's important for Audrey to understand that if we do something she wants to do, it may mean Emma misses out on something *she* was counting on—and vice versa.

All too often parents put their children first. Your initial response may be that this probably doesn't seem like a bad thing. Unfortunately, many parents often put their children's wants ahead of their own—to a fault. As a result, the children become the center of the family, the rulers of family schedules, meals, and everything else.

You know the kind of family I mean. It's the one where the children—or perhaps one child in particular—is deferred to, and around whom the rest of the family sets their schedules: "We can't come for dinner; Johnny has rehearsal." "My schedule is so packed—all of Johnny's classes, you know."

In situations like these there is no balance, no taking into account the other members of the family. And that can be dangerous.

Robert Benson has this to say about balance: "Our lives hang in the balance, one might say. And if there is no balance, then they are indeed hanging by a thread."[25]

The overscheduling of your family may feel out of control, but it is *completely* within your control to change. We have the choice about what our families commit to, what our families are involved in. And as parents, we can say no, set limits, and teach our children the importance of not packing every moment of every day so full there's no room left to breathe.

I like what one mom said when I asked for her opinion on balance: "Something that makes my life so much less complicated than others' is that I keep afterschool activities to a minimum. I don't overschedule my kids at all. My rule is school plus one other activity. I find that not having to run my kids around from points A to B to C makes our lives easier. We are home at a normal hour so that I have time to make dinner and the kids have time to play before homework, showers, and bedtime."

It's okay to say no to our kids when they want to take ballet, learn to play the violin, participate in youth soccer, *and* join the Scouts. We must learn balance ourselves, and then teach our children the value of downtime—the importance of time to think, to ponder, to just be.

Author Madeline L'Engle includes lots of helpful parenting instruction in her book *Walking on Water: Reflections on Faith and Art*. This is what she has to say about children and solitude:

> Allowing the child a certain amount of solitude in a reasonably safe environment (no environment in this world is totally safe) is allowing the child's imagination to grow and develop, so that the child may ultimately learn how to be mature.[26]

I couldn't agree more. I have wonderful memories of being alone as a child, of thinking private thoughts and dreaming private dreams.

When we program our children's lives to death, we rob them of the space needed to gain this kind of maturity. They may be able to sing and dance, to paint and follow the leader, but they will not know how to be alone well or how to use their imaginations. Programmed to the hilt, they become conditioned to being constantly entertained, rather than learning to entertain themselves.

Even when we choose not to overschedule, however, the choices made by other families sometimes affects us. Here is what another mom had to say: "We've intentionally not 'scheduled' our kids in hopes of creating rich childhood memories at home and in our own neighborhood. I just wish it were easier to fit into other people's lives. These days, it's hard to find friends for my kids who are available to 'just play'—not go do something organized, but simply play. To ride bikes, build forts, make up games. But so many people have their kids scheduled into a plethora of 'enrichment activities.'"

Mommy Time

We all need solitude, time to pursue our own interests and ideas. In fact, if you're not regularly taking some time for yourself, you need to. It's best for the whole family if you're rested and happy.

After Emma was born, I went a little nuts. I had a two-year-old and an infant, and I began to wonder where they ended and I began. My life and identity vacillated between "Mommy! Mommy!" from Audrey and nursing Emma (what my brother-in-law calls "the Dairy Queen"). Toben saw the problem and helped me run away from home—for a week to Paris with four girlfriends, to celebrate my thirtieth birthday. (I know, he's really, *really* wonderful!) I came home refreshed, renewed, and knowing who I was as a whole person.

Maybe you can't run away for a week to Paris, but you can pick a night to hang out with your girlfriends or spend some time alone. Start a new hobby (I recommend ballet—you're never too old to wear a tutu, and how cool are leg warmers?) or dive into an old one.

One of my friends scrapbooks, another walks on the beach, and still another takes a bubble bath every night while her husband gets the kids ready for bed. The consensus is, "Without it, I'd go crazy!"

When you've found that time for yourself to recharge and rest, you can go off and do things together—again, taking the opinions of your entire family into account. Let's face it—you're not all going to love everything you do. For example, I don't particularly like miniature golf. But I'll go, because I love being with my family. As you factor in everyone's preferences, you'll find some of that peace by keeping in step with each other. And you *can* draw the line. (For my family, this means no Chuck E. Cheese. Period.)

Cultivating Thankfulness

"And cultivate thankfulness" (Colossians 3:15, *The Message*).

Thankfulness is so important when it comes to living a simple life. Taking the time to be thankful makes me realize how much I have and what's really important. It puts my focus back on God.

So how do we cultivate thankfulness? We might start by looking at what it means to cultivate something. I immediately think of gardening—planting a new seed and watching it grow, pulling weeds, watering regularly, and adding fertilizer.

Thankfulness must be nurtured. Ever notice how, when you stop being thankful and allow "weeds" to crop up, they come back in droves? We have to pull the weeds—those things that crowd thankfulness and keep it from growing. This means we stop complaining, stop focusing on those things we lack.

We can encourage thankfulness to grow by talking about ways to be thankful. Start a list on the fridge and encourage your family to add to it. Share what you're thankful for while you're eating dinner together. Take notice when others are thankful, and comment on it.

Teaching with Scripture

"Let the Word of Christ have the run of the house" (Colossians 3:15, *The Message*).

What does it look like for Scripture to have the run of the house? In my opinion, it means that there's a verse for every situation.

Teach your children to turn to Scripture for help when they need it. Back up your answers to your kids by quoting Scripture to them.

In Jan Karon's series about the tiny town of Mitford, Father Tim's dog, Barnabas—a huge, black, energetic dog—is disciplined by Scripture alone. Shouts of alarm, yelling at him to stop—none of it works on Barnabas. But when Father Tim quotes verses from the Bible, Barnabas ceases whatever naughty prank he is up to and pays attention.

Wouldn't it be great if we were the same way with God?

Maybe your dog won't respond to Scripture, but chances are good your kids will.

Audrey and Emma came into the kitchen one morning, arguing and bickering and generally being awful to each other. I knew that if the day kept going the way it started, we'd all be miserable. I could feel my temper fraying and prayed for God's wisdom. Then the answer popped into my head. "I want you to go find a verse that talks about what it means to be sisters from your verse cards," I told them. "Then I want you to memorize it together. When you've done that, come recite it to me."

I'll admit, I wasn't expecting it to work as well as it did. They tramped grumpily out of the kitchen, and then reemerged thirty minutes later to help each other recite Psalm 133:1: "How good and pleasant it is when [sisters] live together in unity." (They took the liberty of changing the word *brothers* to *sisters*—and I don't think God minded.)

Now before you go thinking that this tactic wouldn't work with your kids in a million years, give it a try. It doesn't always work, but knowing that God has said something to be true automatically gives more weight to my words. Mom saying so isn't always enough.

The following is a list of some of the great verses I've found for my kids. These verses give them confidence when they're feeling afraid, remind them of what God has said to be true, instruct them on how to treat others, and affirm their worth. I've written the verses down on index cards, and the girls have decorated them with stickers—hearts, stars, alphabet stickers that spell out words, happy faces, and so on.

Be joyful always. (1 Thessalonians 5:16)

I will set before my eyes no vile thing. (Psalm 101:3)

A cheerful look brings joy to the heart.
(Proverbs 15:30)

But may the righteous be glad and rejoice before God;
may they be happy and joyful. (Psalm 68:3)

Nothing in all creation is hidden from God's sight.
(Hebrews 4:13)

We love because he first loved us. (1 John 4:19)

Love is patient, love is kind. (1 Corinthians 13:4)

Turn my eyes away from worthless things.
(Psalm 119:37)

Children, obey your parents. (Ephesians 6:1)

I sought the Lord and he answered me; he delivered
me from all my fears. (Psalm 34:4)

Do not let any unwholesome talk come out of your
mouths, but only what is helpful for building others up
according to their needs, that it may benefit those who
listen. (Ephesians 4:29)

I will lie down and sleep in peace, for you alone,
O LORD, make me dwell in safety. (Psalm 4:8)

Whatever your hand finds to do, do it with all your
might. (Ecclesiastes 9:10)

For I am the LORD, your God, who takes hold of your
right hand and says to you, Do not fear; I will help you.
(Isaiah 41:13)

Be devoted to one another in [sisterly] love. Honor one
another above yourselves. (Romans 12:10)

Apply your heart to instruction and your ears to words of knowledge. (Proverbs 23:12)

When I am afraid, I will trust in you. (Psalm 56:3)

Do not worry about tomorrow. (Matthew 6:34)

Encourage one another daily. (Hebrews 3:13)

Let your "Yes" be "Yes," and your "No," "No." (Matthew 5:37)

Let us love one another, for love comes from God. (1 John 4:7)

And the Lord's servant must not quarrel; instead, [she] must be kind to everyone. (2 Timothy 2:24)

Whoever loves God must also love [her sister]. (1 John 4:21)

Give thanks in all circumstances. (1 Thessalonians 5:18)

The Lord detests lying lips, but he delights in [children] who are truthful. (Proverbs 12:22)

Don't grumble against each other. (James 5:9)

Do everything without complaining or arguing. (Philippians 2:14)

How good and pleasant it is when [sisters] live together in unity. (Psalm 133:1)

Learning Common Sense

"Instruct and direct one another using good common sense" (Colossians 3:16, *The Message*).

How open are you to learning from your kids? This isn't an easy one for me as a mother. But I think that every member of the family has something to teach the others.

We tend to think that common sense is an adult trait—something children are lacking by the bucketful. But children are surprisingly logical at times.

"Are you okay, Mom?" Emma asked me one day.

"Yeah, but I have a headache and I'm really tired right now," I responded, wandering listlessly from one thing to the next.

"Then go lie down," she said.

Common sense, indeed.

Sing Your Heart Out

"Sing your hearts out to God!" (Colossians 3:16, *The Message*).

I love to sing—although I don't do it particularly well. What I really love is listening to women who can *sing*. I can't imagine opening my mouth and having something like Christina Aguilera's voice come out. Okay, maybe you don't think she's that great. But I'm amazed that such a big voice comes out of such a petite person. Go ahead and substitute someone you enjoy hearing belt it out, and you'll know what I mean!

How cool would that be? When I get to heaven, one of the things I'm most excited about is to sing beautifully.

I love the last verse of "Amazing Grace":

When we've been there ten thousand years,
Bright, shining as the sun,
We've no less days to sing God's praise
Than when we'd first begun.

In the meantime, we can sing our hearts out to God as best we can. For my family, this usually happens in the car.

I was at a training event for Girl Scouts the other night. One of the trainers grew up in a scouting family and said that her children joke that she knows a song for just about everything. I love that! My mother's best friend was that way, too—she had a song for any and every situation. She even knew one about toothbrushes who fell in love!

Children learn exceptionally well when what they're learning is put to music. I'm always amazed by how quickly a few simple bars from a song on the radio can bring to mind words I haven't sung in years. I'm sure if my chemistry teacher had sung the periodic table I'd have learned it in no time flat!

Wives, Husbands, and Children

In Colossians 3:13–21, Paul gives specific instructions to each of the members of a family—wives, husbands, and children. The verse about wives submitting is a difficult one for many women to understand, but I think Beth Moore does an excellent job explaining it: Paul is not *against* women, she says, but rather *for* order. Paul wants families to function in an orderly way.

At one time I really struggled with not liking this verse. But then I made the choice to believe that God knows what He's talking about (the horrifying alternative: God doesn't know what He's talking about. That's far worse to think about than the idea of submission). To believe that He loves me and knows what's best for me. I'm a fairly black-and-white thinker. Therefore, I can choose to obey this verse—or not.

I love how the Amplified version translates Ephesians 5:33—the other big submission verse. Take a look:

And let the wife see that she respects and reverences her husband—that she notices him, regards him, honors him, prefers him, venerates and esteems him; and that she defers to him, praises him, and loves and admires him exceedingly.

Pretty big undertaking, huh? But I imagine that if I managed to do all that, Toben would have no problem loving me in return—not that he has a hard time loving me now. It's just easier to respond in love to someone who loves you like that, don't you think?

⁓

I'm not a husband, so I don't have a lot to say about the husband's role in a family. But I've heard it said that Paul told women to submit, knowing it was a difficult task for us. At the same time, he told husbands to love their wives, knowing it was a difficult task for them, too.

It's so easy to start comparing roles and jobs, placing each person's tasks and responsibilities on a scale to see whose side comes out weighing more. Too often we want to justify our actions by pointing fingers at the other person.

In Ephesians, Paul instructs husbands to love their wives "just as Christ loved the church and gave himself up for her" (Ephesians 5:25).

No question about it: That's a big task, too.

⁓

One of my favorite verses as a mother is "Children, obey your parents." Just ask Audrey and Emma—it gets quoted to them a lot.

The thing I must be diligent about is finishing the verse—especially as it's stated in *The Message*. Why should they obey?

Because it pleases God—"to no end," even! It's crucial that I help Audrey and Emma understand that they're not meant to obey out of duty or fear of punishment, but to please God. (Of course, it pleases us as parents, too.)

When we love someone, we want to please them, and the chores we do become joy rather than drudgery. Remember doing laundry when your kids were babies? There was such joy in washing tiny socks and shirts, in folding them and putting them away where they belonged. Oh, how I want to regain that attitude of doing chores out of a heart filled with love!

Pursuing Praise

Finally, Paul instructs parents to discipline without crushing.

I've been spending lots of time in Avonlea lately, snuggled in my pajamas reading the *Anne of Green Gables* books. I've always loved Anne, ever since my grandmother visited Nova Scotia and brought me back a green and yellow paperback book with a picture of a red-haired girl on the cover.

Maybe it's because I have red hair, like Anne (although mine could truly be called auburn). Maybe it's because Anne found imaginary friends in echoes and reflections to share adventures and secret thoughts. Whatever the reason, Anne is a very real person to me, and one of the "kindred spirits" of my childhood.

Anne came to my mind just now because I lost my temper yesterday. And Anne had such a struggle with her temper.

I feel my temper rising inside, clawing its way to get out and explode. I know I should tamp it down, grab a piece of paper and scribble away, or lock myself in the bathroom and yell. But it bubbles and churns and there's such a perverse pleasure and relief in letting it boil over to scald those around me. I regret it as soon as it's done, of course. I hate cleaning up after its explosion as much as I dislike scrubbing the mess on the stovetop after a pot has boiled over.

Audrey was the one I burned yesterday. I came down hard and saw the look in her eyes as her spirit was crushed. I could make excuses: "Yes, but I was tired, I was fighting a cold, my ears hurt, I was already frustrated by the girls' arguing and whining." The list could go on.

Isn't it awful how many poor choices we make? We don't like the busyness, the excess, the "ships passing in the night" habits of our families. But we chose it. "I didn't choose this," you and I argue. But not choosing *is* choosing.

So what's the opposite of crushing? Elevating. Praising. Building up. Inflating. Filling.

I think most parents have heard the instruction that for every negative comment you make to your child you should make five positive ones. Or is it ten? Whatever the number, the idea works.

Why are the things that stand out in our minds and memories not the positive comments or the compliments? Instead, the things that demand our attention, that pop up at unexpected moments, seem to be the negative things, the hurtful things.

I want to do a better job of praising my children. It came more naturally when they were smaller and learning so many new things. Sitting up, clapping hands, saying "mama," taking a step or two on wobbly legs—those things were praised with exclamations of joy and retold to anyone who would listen. The checkout lady at the grocery store knew when Audrey walked, when Emma talked. And everyone knew when they made it out of diapers!

As my daughters get older, some of those everyday accomplishments go unnoticed—or at least unpraised. Making the bed is expected. I notice when it's done but rarely comment on it. Brushing teeth is expected. Not big enough to merit praise.

But should they leave those things undone—well, then I have a comment or two or three.

Why is it that I stopped praising them so frequently? I certainly appreciate it when someone notices something I've done well. I doubt my children are any different.

When was the last time you praised your child to other people—in your child's presence? I bet your child stood a little taller, looked a bit uncomfortable, and maybe even complained, "Moooom!" But the grin on that sweet face told you how much it really meant.

Just last week, Audrey finally passed a timed test in math. The students pass one and move onto the next level with some frequency. But this level threw her for a loop, and we'd been working on it for months. She came down the hill to the carpool line brimming with excitement. When she told me her news, I jumped up and down and screamed like a little girl.

"Mooooom!" Audrey yelled over my screaming.

But she was grinning from ear to ear, and I could tell she was secretly thrilled by my reaction.

Tell Me Some More About Your Family

When it comes to family, my mother has been such an example for me—during my childhood, for sure, but especially since I became a mother myself.

I spend lots of time reflecting on my own childhood: the memories I have, the things I loved, the things I didn't like so much. I look back on my memories not only to glimpse my own experience, but also to remember how my mother dealt with everything from discipline to free time to taking care of her own needs.

I think family is a wonderful thing, and I love hearing about other people's families. The memories they have from childhood, the traditions, the fun jokes they share. How they keep in touch, and what makes them unique. I suppose you could call it nosy, but I just love knowing all about other people.

Imagine if we all shared the wonderful things that make our families so special. We'd have many great ideas to choose from when building our own families. I've found one such family to admire in the *Betsy-Tacy* books. Like the character Joe, I love the Ray family:

> "While we're waiting for that fudge to harden," said Joe, "tell me some more about your family." He liked to hear about the traditions, the holidays, the family jokes, and the simple everyday doings of the Rays.[27]

The Rays represent the kind of family I want us to be. They are always welcoming; others are drawn to their family and want to be part of it.

Think about your family and other families you know. Talk with your girlfriends. Share your ideas. Invest in your family.

But the nicest present she received was not the
usual kind of present. It was the present of a friend.[28]

Simple Friendship

LUCY MAUD MONTGOMERY FIRST PUT INTO WORDS FOR me the longing I experienced for a friend. As I read about how her young heroine, Anne Shirley, made up imaginary friends in bookcase reflections and echoes, I felt her longing keenly. I understood at once the desire for that kind of friend—a bosom friend. A friend with whom you can share everything.

I was thrilled for Anne when Marilla told her that the Barry family across the pond had a girl about her age. I hoped along with Anne that she would find a kindred spirit in Diana. I watched them as they swore to be friends to each other for "as long as the sun and moon shall endure."

I wandered with Anne and Diana through Lover's Lane and drifted with them in Mr. Barry's skiff upon the Lake of Shining Waters. I ran alongside them through the Haunted Wood; their fear of white things in the night was mine, too. I felt their sorrow when, after Diana drank too much red currant wine, Mrs. Barry refused to let them be friends (Anne served the wine to Diana at tea, mistakenly thinking it was raspberry cordial).

I was delighted when, as adults, Diana named her small daughter Anne Cordelia and Anne named her own twin girls Anne and Diana.

Anne and Diana remained true to their original vow of friendship throughout their lives, even though they were separated by many miles as adults.

Despite feeling myself a part of their sacred friendship, I longed for a Diana of my own. (With my red hair and temper, I knew I was more of an Anne!) But because my father was in the Air Force, we moved often and friendships were hard to maintain across an ocean.

Yes, I had friends—best friends—during those three- or four-year periods we lived in one place. Jenny was my dearest friend as a young child, and always bowed to my more bossy nature. My mother still has a picture of Jenny standing in our kitchen doorway, dripping wet. "Why are you all wet, Jenny?" she asked. "Joanne made me wash my hair" was Jenny's response.

Nichole and another Jenny were my dearest friends during my early elementary school years. Thinking of them conjures memories of riding our bikes and climbing the huge rock formations behind our house. We lived in the foothills of the Rocky Mountains at the time, and the scrub oak woods behind our house and down the valley were dotted with giant rock formations. We named every one—Monster Rock, King's Crown, Ghost Rock. Our friendship grew with the fresh air.

Fifth grade brought another move, and with it Janet came into my life. She and I played in her mother's makeup drawer and thought up elaborate, soap-opera-worthy storylines for our Barbie dolls. When I came down with the chicken pox, Janet's mother sent her over every afternoon in hopes that she would catch it, too. She did, and our families spent a weekend camping together—four adults and their Calamine lotion–dotted children.

Heidi and I became friends after we moved to England. We had our first crush together—on Michael J. Fox, after seeing *Back to the Future*. We took horseback riding lessons and spent hours dreaming about growing up and falling in love. We wore dangly earrings and blue eye shadow when our mothers weren't looking, and we loved each other faithfully—even when Heidi switched schools to attend Queen Ethelburga's.

My family eventually moved back to the States, and there were new friends—Kelly, Linda, and Ann, among others—but it was different. It seemed harder to become bosom friends as we hung out at the mall and worried about how we looked.

Who are the friends of your childhood? What do you remember of your time together? Do you still keep in touch? My first friend, Jenny, and I have seen each other several times as adults—and I always love getting a Christmas card from her.

Kindred Spirits

As Anne Shirley grew into adulthood, she discovered that kindred spirits are more easily found than she thought. I've discovered the same to be true. Gone is much of the worry over what other people think; in its place is an ability to be real and accept others as they are.

I don't think it was until after college that I really came into the kind of friendships I'd been looking for all along. The handful of friends I hold most dear are friends I've had for a while now—they know me pretty close to completely and have been my lifeline in hard times. We are all different—divorced, single, married, mothers—and we each bring something valuable to the friendship. These are women I trust with my most secret self, women I trust with my children, women I want to be like.

As we get older, it seems that friendship naturally becomes simpler. I watch Audrey and the girls in my Brownie troop and the kids on the playground at lunch, and I smile at all the drama that goes on. Friends argue and make up, getting everyone around them involved in the process. Others worry and plan about who will sit where on the bus ride home. Feelings are hurt because someone else took the name they wanted for the imaginary game of the hour.

There's not much drama in my friendships these days. And that's fine with me. I don't want friendships in which I'm never really sure where I stand or if the other person might have their feelings hurt. I care about my friends' feelings, to be sure, but I'd rather they just call me on something than fret and stew over how—or if—to approach me.

I watched part of the film *Connie and Carla* yesterday. At one point in the film, Carla turns to Connie and said, "You've been really weird. Just stop it!"

I'm lucky to have friends like Carla—friends who aren't afraid to tell me the truth for my own good, friends who want to help me be the best I can be. I appreciate my friends' honesty—though I don't always like what they have to say. I trust that they know me, love me, and want what is best for me.

⁘

Moving away from my closest friends to California was hard. As I contemplated having to make new friends in a new place, it scared me to think that my old friendships might end.

But as my friend Hanna says, "I have friends—they just don't live here!" So, because we don't live near one another anymore, we make time together a priority. Twice a year we convene for "girl time": a long weekend to catch up, knit, shop, cry, laugh, and be friends face-to-face.

These times together are essential for the rest of my life. After Emma was born, I went a little bit crazy, as I've said before. With a toddler and an infant, I felt trapped at home, always needed by someone for something. My life was reduced to only one part of me, and the rest of me felt stifled. That was when Toben encouraged me to spend a week with my girlfriends in Paris.

That week away reminded me that I'm more than a mother. It also helped me realize that in order for me to be the best mother I can be, the other parts of me need to be nurtured. I came home resolved to make time with friends a priority and a regular part of my life.

So we signed up for a ballet class together and spent every Tuesday night doing pliés, learning how to pirouette, and mastering the proper way to curtsy. We'd finish those evenings by going out for a late dinner of bacon and eggs, tea and sympathy.

As we ate and talked and laughed and cried, we all cherished each moment, the way you do when you know something is special and uncommon and must be remembered for always.

I came across a quote from C. S. Lewis the other day that I love. In a letter to his best friend, Arthur Greeves, Lewis wrote:

> Friendship is the greatest of worldly goods. Certainly to me it is the chief happiness of life. If I had to give advice to a young man about a place to live, I think I [should] say "sacrifice almost everything to live where you can be near your friends."[29]

I agree. But that's not always possible.

Carry Each Other's Burdens

Why do I need friends? Why do I say so often that I couldn't live without these women in my life? Because there are times when the load is too heavy to bear on my own. I stagger under its weight and drop to my knees, unable to stand without help.

That's where friendship comes in. In Galatians 6:2, the apostle Paul tells us to "carry each other's burdens" in order to fulfill the law Jesus gave of loving our neighbor as ourselves.

It's worth noting the difference between burdens and loads. A load is made up of our everyday concerns. The normal, day-to-day stuff of life. Things like taking the kids to the doctor for a check-up, lunch duty once a month, finding something healthy to cook for dinner.

A burden is something that's beyond our normal concerns. A burden is taking the kids to the doctor for a check up when your car breaks down, lunch duty when you're too sick to get out of bed, finding something healthy to cook for dinner when you've just had a baby.

In general, I'm a pretty independent person, and in the past I've had a hard time asking for help. I don't like to admit I can't do it—whatever *it* is—on my own. I've always been much more likely to skip ahead to verse 5, where Paul says that "each one should carry his own load." That's always been easier for me.

But when we moved to California—far away from family and friends—and Toben was diagnosed as being bipolar, I found myself beneath a burden I couldn't bear. His crisis—of health, of faith, of love, of family, of life itself—became my crisis, too. And the questions, sorrow, doubts, fears, and exhaustion of it all pressed down on me with a weight unlike anything I'd ever felt before. This burden sat on my chest and pushed down so hard that I could barely breathe. I was suffocating and faced a choice—to slowly die on my own under the weight of it or to call for help.

I let go of my pride, my pretense, my perfection and admitted to my friends that I was unable to...what? To live, to function, to parent, to love...to do anything without their help.

Like superheroes, they flew to my rescue—literally. Sarah flew to California for thirty-six hours to babysit my children while I went with Toben to a memorial service and to listen to my questions and fears and to hold me while I cried. Emily regularly called to tell me she loved me and supported me. She took my side in everything and let me know she stood by me with unwavering loyalty. Michelle prayed faithfully for me and my husband and my children, lifting us up before the One most able—completely able—to help.

These women gathered around me and grabbed a corner of my burden. They helped me stand up, shouldered some of the weight, and huddled around me as we began to shuffle step by step down the path. Can you see it? It was like they all took a part of this huge, heavy thing and crab-walked with me until my burden began to shrink, until my own strength returned, until I could stand up straight again.

∞

We got an e-mail from a friend yesterday telling us that he and his wife are getting divorced. They are one of those rare families that we really connected with once upon a time. Audrey and their oldest daughter are the same age and loved to play together. She and I were pregnant together with our second children, and the two girls found comfort in each other when it was time to go off to Sunday school alone. I was in a Bible study with her; Toben was in a Bible study with him. We love their family dearly.

Though we lost touch with them when we moved away, they have remained dear friends—the kind you can pick up with right where you left off, no matter how much time has passed since you saw each other last.

We knew they were struggling. We knew they had separated for a time. But the news that divorce is imminent struck hard. I have wept for them and prayed for their family. I spent the past few hours wondering if I did not pray hard enough, often enough, or with the right words.

My heart grieves for my friend; she is now a single mother and has to explain to her small children why Daddy moved out, moved to another town. My heart grieves for her children; I look ahead to when this sad period of time will be the defining memory of their childhoods. And my heart grieves for the husband; he has suffered in such a way that this feels like the only option.

How can I be a friend in such a time?

Lifting Each Other Up

I just finished reading Robert Benson's book *Living Prayer* for the umpteenth time. It is one of those books that I read again and again. Months go by and one day it's just time to read it again, afresh.

I love books like that.

In one of the chapters near the end, he wonders how to pray for others. Intercessory prayer is the theological name for it, I suppose. How do we pray for someone going through something devastating? What can we tell God about or ask Him for that He doesn't already know or anticipate?

As much as I like answers and those movies in which the ending is tied up neatly without any loose ends, it's comforting to know that some of the people we admire and emulate ask the same questions we do. "I am not sure that any of us ever quite knows how to pray when it is time to pray for others," Benson writes. But, he agrees, pray we must.

> To lift up those who have been given to us, and to whom we have been given, is all, and possibly, everything, that we can do.... So we lift them up, sharing some bit of the burden and hoping and praying that someone else is shouldering a bit of it too, so that the burdens can be lifted, or failing that, at least carried somehow by us all, if we will carry them together the way we have been called to do.[30]

And so, not knowing what or how to pray for this family, I can only lift them up, one by one, to the God who loves and cares for them more than I do. I lift them up each day, as "those we know who face particular trials this day" as the prayer book says. I lift them up, believing that by doing so, the promise of God will be fulfilled as He "daily bears our burdens" (Psalm 68:19).

Any friend can help you out in a pinch. But only a believing friend can lift you up before God.

Modeling Friendship

My daughter Audrey is in the second grade this year and is learning what it means to be a friend. She's had friends thus far in school, but for the first time she's finding the joy of having a best friend. It's something, childhood development experts assure me, that children learn around this age.

But there are a lot of girls in Audrey's second-grade class—about three quarters of the kids are girls. And with the joy of "best" friendship, the girls are also learning what it means to be left out. Notes have been passed back and forth, notes saying things like "I don't want to play with you" and "You're not my friend" and "I don't like you." Children at this age don't seem to understand that being friends with one person doesn't mean you can't be friends with anyone else.

"She and I aren't friends anymore, Mom," Audrey said one day after school about a girl in her class.

"Why not? Did you have a fight?" I asked.

"No. But we don't sit together on the bus anymore and we don't play at recess," she answered.

We talked some more and I tried to explain to Audrey that just because she wants to play tetherball and another girl wants to swing on the monkey bars doesn't mean that they're not friends. Yes, friends share similar interests. But they also have different ones. The world would be pretty monotonous if we all were the same.

She's doubtful about that. Which is something else the experts say is normal.

So how do we teach our children about friendship?

Kids learn by example. What do they see in your friendships? Are you too busy to nurture a friendship, or do you make friendship a priority? Do your kids see you laugh and cry with your friends? Do they see you pray for and support your friends? Do they see the love you have for your friends?

"I'll call again soon. I love you. Bye!" I ended my conversation with Emily and turned to find Audrey looking at me.

"You *love* her, Mom?" She's heard me say this to friends before, but this was the first time she commented on it.

"Of course. She's my friend!" I went on to explain that love isn't just about boys and girls (*"Ooooh...gross!"* she says, and shudders) and families, the way it is in Audrey's seven-year-old head.

◠

Just the other day, a group of moms sat around my living room and talked about friendships and best-friendships. There's an ideal of having one best friend that seems to come naturally to kids—or at least to little girls. (I don't have little boys in my life, so I just don't know about them!) But we talked about the importance of having lots of friends, a wide circle of friends. If Audrey and her best friend are playing together, that's fine. What's not fine is excluding anyone else. As moms, we want our girls (somehow it seems to be something girls struggle with more than boys) to be friends with everybody.

I pray for my girls to have friends as they grow up, and that their friends would be good friends, not bad friends. Have you ever had a bad friend? I had a bad friend once—she influenced me to do things I knew I shouldn't do, and I wasn't strong enough to say no. I did things for her approval, things that put myself and others in danger. Things that I was uncomfortable with, but did anyway. Things that got me grounded—for months.

I'm always proud to hear that Audrey stayed behind to comfort a girl who felt left out, rather than follow her friends and go along with the crowd. I want to let her know how wonderful it is that she knows herself well enough and is strong enough to stand up for herself. The other day she said she played by herself at recess. "Why didn't you play with your friends?" I asked. "They were playing tetherball," she said. "And I just didn't feel like it today."

I gave her a hug and told her I was proud of her for knowing what she wanted to do. "You don't always have to do what everyone else does," I encouraged her.

Believing Friends

I'd never really thought of the "unequally yoked" thing in terms of friendship before. It was always something pulled out to back up my parents' rule against dating non-Christian boys. Unequally yoked seemed to be strictly for boy-girl stuff.

The *one* time I brought home a non-Christian boy was a horrible enough experience that I never tried it again. I laugh about it now—it's funny to think of Brian's face going completely blank when my dad interrupted a conversation about Brian's astronomy class to ask him, "So, Brian, if you were to die tonight and stand before the gates of heaven and God were to say, 'Why should I let you into my heaven?'—what would you say?"

It was *not* funny at the time! My parents let us go out, but I stopped Brian outside the front door and told him I understood if he no longer wanted to take me to dinner. He still did…but that was our last date.

I pray through *The Power of a Praying Parent* for my girls each month, and I was recently struck by something Stormie Omartian wrote:

> God's Word clearly instructs us: "Do not be unequally yoked together with unbelievers. For what fellowship has righteousness with lawlessness? And what communion has light with darkness?... Or what part has a believer with an unbeliever?" (2 Corinthians 6:14–15). That doesn't mean our children can never have a nonbelieving friend. But there is clear implication that their closest friends, the ones to whom they have strong ties, should be believers. "Can two walk together unless they are agreed?" (Amos 3:3). No, they can't. That means if they are not agreed, somebody has to change. And that's why "The righteous should choose his friends carefully, for the way of the wicked leads them astray" (Proverbs 12:26).[31]

What's true for our children is true for us, too. A simple friendship is a friendship that starts with a believing friend. (Yes, I do want to know non-Christian women, too, and to share the love of Jesus with them. But my dearest friends are those who share my faith.)

The book of Proverbs is filled with instruction about friendship. Perhaps the verse we most often think about when it comes to friendship is Proverbs 27:17, about iron sharpening iron. Take a look at how it reads in *The Message*: "You use steel to sharpen steel, and one friend sharpens another."

I want believing friends who will sharpen me, who will challenge me and gently help me see those things in myself that need to be changed. I want friends who will challenge me to continue to grow in God.

I want friends who are walking down the same path, not pulling me in another direction. I want friends whom I aspire to be like. I find myself looking for women I can admire and look up to and follow. I want to be a prayer warrior like Michelle, interested in new ideas like Sarah, creative and full of fun like Terri, truthful like Hanna, brave like Emily.

I want friends my girls will admire and emulate, too.

Heading to Gayle's House

Nowadays it seems like everyone is called by their first name. It wasn't really until Audrey started school that I became Mrs. Heim.

Now, after a year of teaching art and another of leading a Brownie troop, I actually respond pretty quickly to "Mrs. Heim" without first looking around for Toben's mother.

Gayle was the first of my mother's friends that I was allowed to call by her first name. She was the first of my mother's friends to be one of my friends, too.

To get to Gayle's house, you had to go down our very long and steep driveway, down the very long and steep cul-de-sac, and then turn left and head down the street before turning left again and heading up the hill. It was a good eight- or ten-minute walk—especially since I was a kid and stopped to look at interesting things along the way.

There was a shortcut, of course. I could go out the garage, jump across a little hidden spot between two rocks, and take the path that wound down to Monster Rock. Around it and past Ghost Rock, through a scrub oak patch, and out onto the sidewalk across the street from Gayle's house.

The first time my mom figured out how to French braid my hair—in two braids, with the ends tucked up underneath and tied with ribbons—I took the shortcut to show Gayle. Gayle had two boys and I figured she needed some girly stuff in her life.

It was Gayle who first did my colors when *Color Me Beautiful* came out, which showed me that I look better in brown than red. Of course, I love red—and pink!—and wear them all the time now despite my red hair. Some "rules" are just meant to be broken.

It was Gayle who helped my mother rearrange the furniture with some frequency and who gave me my first babysitting job. I think she paid me in quarters and popsicles.

To be allowed to call her Gayle made me feel like such a grown-up. So it was to Gayle I ran when my parents didn't understand, Gayle whose advice I sought when my mom was unavailable or unyielding.

I look at my friends now and see them as Audrey and Emma's "Gayles." I guess that's why it's so important to me that my dearest friends share my faith. These women are not just my friends; I hope they will be my daughters' friends, too. Because these women share my beliefs and my values, I know that they can be trusted to guide my girls "in the way they should go," as Proverbs 22:6 says, when Audrey and Emma run to them for help and advice.

Though we share a common faith, my friends and I have different backgrounds and different experiences. Audrey and Emma won't have to take my word for everything; they can go ask one of my friends who chose differently than I did. Advice on dating, college, career, marriage, sex, and family— because of my circle of friends, Audrey and Emma will have all kinds of different experiences to listen to, to learn from, to follow.

I know that my children will not always come to me first. As much as I'd like to believe otherwise, it's true! They'll go to their friends (and oh, how I pray for those friends!) and to my friends. The day will come when they'll ask for someone else's advice before mine.

Friends for a Season and Friends for Life

I think friends can be divided into two groups—friends for a season and friends for life. Looking at all the friends in my life, I'm sometimes surprised by which is which.

Friends for a season are those friends close to us when our lives intersect at a certain point—a child's preschool, living in a certain neighborhood, sharing a similar interest.

Friends for life are those friends that we are connected to despite divergent interests, distance, or time. They are the kinds of friends with whom you can just pick up where you left off without any awkwardness.

Both kinds of friends are important, both kinds of friends can sharpen, both kinds of friends are wonderful to have.

So how do we keep those friendships simple?

Maybe it all comes back to the Golden Rule: *Do unto others as you would have done to you.*

What kinds of friends do you want in your life? Give that question some thought—and then set about to be that kind of friend.

When Audrey was born, I couldn't help but notice that some of the best gifts came from women who had children of their own. The same was true when Emma was born. The best gifts often came from mothers who had more than one child. They were the ones who made sure to include Audrey in their gifts with a little something to make her feel special. They were the ones who paid attention to her, getting down on her level, *before* rushing over to *ooh* and *ahh* over her new little sister.

I learned from them. And after my sister had her first baby, I delighted in sending her little gifties in the mail—just something small, to remind her that she was loved. I remembered so well how after everyone comes by to see the baby, life goes on as usual for others but still feels new and uncertain to a first-time mom. (Besides, who doesn't love getting unexpected presents in the mail?)

Do you want your friends to call and let you know they love you? Then call them and do the same!

Do you want your friends to write you real letters—the kind that come in envelopes, on real stationery? Then do the same for them!

Do you want your friends to invite you out for lunch, to invite your family over for dinner? Then do it yourself!

Do you want your friends to drop by to say hello when they're in the neighborhood? Invite them and do the same to them (although you may want to call first!). I stopped by my friend Terri's house after running some errands the other day. We sat on the couch for a quick half-hour and looked at pictures from her recent vacation. It wasn't planned, wasn't long, wasn't really any big deal—but it made my day.

Do you want your friends to pray for you? Then pray for them. Perhaps this, more than any other thing, demonstrates friendship for one another.

> What binds us together is the prayer, the promise and the lifting of each other's burdens, the commitment we have made, and kept, to be companions to each other on the road that we share. What binds us together is the laying down of our lives for each other in a way that we cannot even explain.[32]

And while we do this, we model friendship to our children, teaching them to do the same.

As I've mentioned, I get together with a group of my closest friends at least once a year. At one time, we all lived in the same town, saw each other at least once a week for Bible study or ballet class or lunch or whatever. I look back on that time and realize how fortunate we were.

Since that time, two of us have moved away to different places, but our friendship has remained strong. We call, we e-mail, we send each other surprise gifts in the mail. But, still, there's nothing like face-to-face time.

And so, about once or twice a year when we all start feeling desperate, we plan a weekend together. It doesn't really matter where we go; the main stipulation is that we be together. We stay up late, eat croissants and drink coffee, wear our pajamas all day, shop, knit, laugh a lot, act totally silly, cry, and just bask in the joy of being together.

We're all different. Some of us have children; others don't. We come from different backgrounds, have different stories. We love each other, challenge each other, and pray for each other.

I can't say enough about how much these women mean to me. I love them. It's as simple and complex and wonderful as that.

Oh, how I encourage you to make your friendships a priority. It's so worth it. Maybe you've been waiting for a friend to take the initiative; maybe you're afraid your friends might say no. Do it anyway!

Perhaps you don't have a group of friends who are all friendly with each other. If not, introduce them to each other. I love to look around and see my friends become friends with one another. To see my friend from college love my neighbor. My friend from church love my friend from college.

Plan a party. Begin a book club. Start a Bible study. Do

something—anything—to bring together the women you know and love.

Start today.

⌁

It seems that we have abandoned the richness found in friendships—in sharing our lives with other women and families—in the busyness that surrounds us. Friendship has been pushed to the side, fit in here and there when we have a moment to spare. We're missing out!

Any relationship must be pursued, nurtured, developed. We *need* friendship. It's not a luxury but a necessity, and it deserves our time and effort and energy. We were created for relationship, created to need others. Husbands and children are wonderful, but they can't meet all of our needs. We need other women!

Do you have "girl time" in your life? If not, you need it. Trust me, you *need* it. Grab a girlfriend and...

- head to the spa
- get a pedicure
- meet for coffee
- go see a chick flick
- go out for lunch
- sign up for a class to learn something new
- knit (one of my favorites!)
- take a walk
- talk on the phone

Your life will be richer for the time and effort spent. Especially as we pursue simplicity, we need friends.

Not many of us have folks around us who are encouraging us to say no in order to say yes to the very most important stuff.[33]

How true these words are! Let's be friends who encourage one another to say yes to the "very most important stuff."

Being God's Friend

When I think about friendship, I also think of being a friend of God.

Moses and Abraham were both called friends of God. James 2:23 says, "'Abraham believed God, and it was credited to him as righteousness,' and he was called God's friend." Exodus 33:11 tells us, "The LORD would speak to Moses face to face, as a man speaks with his friend."

I want to be a friend of God, too. So what does it take?

Jesus says that we can be His friend—but like all friendships, it doesn't just happen. "You are my friends if you do what I command" (John 15:14). That's an awfully big *if*—one we'd prefer to ignore at times.

The cost of being a friend of God is obedience.

As we've been studying the patriarchs in my Bible study group, the idea of obedience has stood out to me. Abraham left his country, his people, and his home without understanding why or what was coming next; he did it because God told him to.

I often tell my children, "Obey first and ask questions later." I tell them that I know more than they do, can see what they can't see, and that they need to trust that I have good reason for telling them to do something. I say this so often that my friend Natalie laughed at me the other day and remarked that it will be one of those sayings my children remember about me as they grow up.

(One of the phrases I remember from my mother is this one: "Be sweet, remember your manners, and don't forget to put on clean underwear." It's one she *still* says laughingly to Kristen and me when we head out the door of her house. And even though she laughs, I'm pretty sure she still means every word.)

Obey Him first and ask questions later. That's the kind of obedience God is looking for. The kind of obedience that prompts Him to call us His friend. To believe that He knows more than we do, that He can see what we can't see. And to trust that He has a good reason for telling us to do something.

To obey God—to be His friend—means choosing obedience over our own way. Choosing what may not make sense because it is what He commands.

And so we're back to the importance of having friends who are believers—friends that will sharpen us as we follow God, friends that will encourage us to say no to some things "in order to say yes to the very most important stuff."

We need friends—plain and simple.

Bless our friends, bless our food.
Come, O Lord, and sit with us.

A Simple Meal

IF HOME IS WHERE OUR FAMILIES ARE CENTERED, then the kitchen is the heart of the home.

My first kitchen was hardly big enough to be called a kitchen. It was smaller than your average walk-in closet and held a mini-fridge, a tiny oven, four burners (incapable of being lit all at once), a miniscule sink, and about eighteen square inches of counter space. It was a tiny part of our tiny first apartment on campus after we got married.

But I loved that apartment. It was the first place I'd ever lived that was really mine.

I loved vacuuming the carpet, dusting our furniture, and, yes, even cleaning the tiny bathroom. When I look back on it, I think of that time as playing house, learning to do laundry, to cook, to get along together as husband and wife.

It was the only kitchen I've had where it was truly impossible for people to gather. Only one person could fit at a time!

My next kitchen was bigger, and that's when I learned that everyone hangs out in the kitchen. Each kitchen subsequently got a little bigger—and now my kitchen is nearly perfect. It's an L-shaped room with space for an eating nook, a coffee table, and a couch. Since people are always in the kitchen while I'm cooking, I figured I'd give them a comfortable place to sit down. The only thing missing is a fireplace and a rocking chair.

Sharing Life over a Meal

After we got married, we were part of a couples' Bible study. Since none of us had children and few of the couples had family in town, we became family for each other. We helped one another move from apartments to first homes, we celebrated holidays together, we called each other when we faced unexpected expenses and ran short of cash.

We loved to read about the early church in Acts and how they shared so much in common—even meals. And so we began to eat dinner together before Bible study. On Thursday nights, everyone showed up at our house an hour before Bible study and gathered around our tiny table. We used every chair we owned!

Each couple brought part of the meal, and when we put it all together, the meal was complete. Tacos, pizzas, omelets, burgers, chili—we had fun planning meals with lots of ingredients that could be assembled quickly.

We held hands around the table to bless our meal and caught up on our lives—triumphs, disappointments, all the everyday little details. We shared life over those simple meals, and our friendships deepened and grew strong.

I love to eat.

What I don't love is eating in a hurry. As a result, I don't love to eat fast food (with the exception of McDonald's French fries and bean burritos from Taco Bell).

I also don't love to eat in the car. Nor do I love to eat lima beans or black-eyed peas.

But I do love to eat chocolate. And ice cream. (I especially loved when I was pregnant and could balance a bowl of ice cream on my belly while I sat in bed. I did this just about every night while pregnant with Audrey—Toben and I joke that God made her with a piece of me, a piece of Toben, and a lot of Rocky Road ice cream.)

I love to eat together as a family, sitting down at the table with candles lit.

I love to eat scrambled eggs with cream cheese and chives—on a toasted bagel, if one is handy.

I love to eat slowly.

I love to eat when I'm good and hungry and the house has smelled of pot roast all afternoon.

I wholeheartedly agree with something Virginia Woolf once wrote: "One cannot think well, love well, sleep well, if one has not dined well."[34] God made us to require food—and the better the food, the greater the pleasure.

Fortunately, I also love to cook—when I have the time to plan and shop, chop and sauté. But I live in the same world you do, and finding the time is not always easy. So we don't eat as gourmet as we used to—no more setting things on fire or standing at the stove to stir and stir and stir and stir the risotto.

But I'm learning that there's more to mealtime than what's on the plate.

Learning to Cook

Recently I was reading the last book in the *Betsy-Tacy* series by Maud Hart Lovelace. By this time Betsy and Joe are married, and Betsy has set up housekeeping. One afternoon her younger sister and her sister's friend, Louisa, stop by after school. I laughed out loud at their conversation:

> "And I heard you say, Betsy, that you didn't know how to cook when you got married. I suppose that after you get married you just sort of know how, automatically. Is that it? You're married, and so you're keeping house and so naturally you know how to cook. Is that the way it is?" And Louisa opened wide, enquiring eyes.
>
> "Well, sort of!" Betsy said.[35]

"Sort of," exactly!

I must admit that I thought I would just "sort of know how" to cook once I got married, too. Never mind the fact that up until our wedding day, I'd only successfully made macaroni and cheese (from a box) and all kinds of ramen noodles. Even scrambled eggs were beyond me.

Like Betsy, I carefully set the table for dinner each night, arranging our new dishes just so and folding the napkins into soft swan-shaped sculptures. I lit candles and played music. And I experimented in the kitchen, trying to figure out what the cookbooks were actually instructing me to do. Clearly, I didn't always understand correctly. I guess I thought that a pretty table would make the food taste better. I was wrong.

And like Betsy's Joe, Toben cheerfully ate whatever I'd cooked and patiently waited for me to learn to cook, hoping it would be sooner than later. After all, you can only eat so much canned tomato soup and so many grilled cheese sandwiches.

Family Dinners

For many families, the image of a family sitting down to dinner together to eat and talk about their days seems old-fashioned and outdated—something from a black-and-white episode of *Leave It to Beaver*. With busy schedules and outside activities, eating together as a family has become the exception, rather than the rule, for many of us. Days go by and we can easily feel like ships passing in the night, roommates who share a roof and little else. As children grow up and begin to lead lives of their own, it's easy for families to feel disconnected.

I think there's something wonderful about meals eaten together. Have you noticed how many references there are in Scripture to the importance God places on meals, or when a meal was the setting for a story? The smell of roasting meat and bread was the scent of fellowship that included forgiveness, peace, celebration, and thanksgiving.

Jesus was always eating with friends—at the home of Mary, Martha, and Lazarus; with Zacchaeus after he came down from his perch in the branches; with His disciples in the upper room before His death; and while roasting fish on the shore for hungry fishermen. At a meal, Jesus taught service to others by washing their feet, Mary anointed Jesus' feet with perfume, and Jesus demonstrated His abundant provision as He fed crowds of people with next to nothing.

❦

I love the words of the *Shema*, found in the book of Deuteronomy. I can see Moses standing above the people, calling to them in a loud voice and instructing them in the ways and laws of Yahweh as they get ready to enter the Promised Land, a land flowing with milk and honey. Someone blows the *shofar*, the ram's horn, and as the sound of it fades and the people look up expectantly, Moses calls out, "Hear, O Israel!" The last few whispers die and Moses waits until everyone is still and ready to listen.

> The LORD our God, the LORD is one. Love the LORD your God with all your heart and with all your soul and with all your strength. These commandments that I give you today are to be upon your hearts. Impress them on your children. Talk about them when you sit at home and when you walk along the road, when you lie down and when you get up. Tie them as symbols on your hands and bind them on your foreheads. Write them on the doorframes of your houses and on your gates. (Deuteronomy 6:4–9)

Talking about God and following His commands were the stuff of everyday life to God's people. It's what they talked about as they went through their days. Everything—every errand, every task, every situation—pointed them back to who God is and how to follow Him.

As a mom, I just love this. It reminds me that teaching my children about God isn't just for Sundays or when they do wrong or when they say their prayers at night. It's for when we are driving in the car and see a beautiful rainbow (the story of Noah), when we're out in the dark and see the stars (the story of Abraham or the words of Isaiah that tell us God calls each star by name), when we're brushing or braiding hair (the fact that God knows exactly how many hairs are on our heads), when they're arguing about who's the best at whatever they're doing (the story of the disciples arguing about who would be first in God's kingdom), or when the wind shakes the trees during a storm (the psalmist's description of the trees clapping their hands for God).

Teaching my children about God is also for mealtimes—when we sit at home around the table together.

The Benefits of Family Dinner

I recently came across a bit of interesting information about eating together as a family.

According to a report from The National Center on Addiction and Substance Abuse (CASA) at Columbia University, how often a family eats dinner together is a strong indicator of whether a teen is likely to smoke, drink, or use drugs, and also whether the teen is likely to perform better academically.[36]

That amazes me. Does it surprise you, too? It tells me that if I want my children to refrain from smoking, drinking, and using drugs, if I want my children to do well in school, then *we need to sit down to dinner as a family*.

The article didn't mention whether those family-centric meals are eaten at home or in a restaurant, but I'd like to think that meals at home have a stronger positive effect than meals eaten out. Eating in a restaurant is great, but there are constant interruptions, worries about whether the children are behaving, people around to watch, other conversations to listen to.

Dinnertime Memories

When I stop to think about it, I realize that many of my childhood memories are from mealtimes.

We didn't eat out very often, but when we did, it was special. For a while, we went to Furr's cafeteria every Sunday after church (mmm...fried okra!). There was also the occasional special breakfast out with Dad at Denny's, my reward for having read twenty books. (The breakfast incentive started out for reading ten books, but once we began going out two to three times a month, Dad upped the number of books.) There were the rare trips to Denver for Mexican food at Casa Bonita—a huge restaurant with a waterfall and divers and a man in a gorilla suit and sopaipillas that came hot and fresh each time you raised the flag at your table.

For the most part, however, we ate at home. Kristen and I took turns setting the table, Mom cooked, and we sat down to dinner when Dad got home from work at 5:30. It was at the dinner table that we learned manners—which fork to use for salad, and to say "please" when you asked someone to pass the mashed potatoes.

On Sundays our family often invited company over after church—missionaries, other families, lonely grandparents. It was during these Sunday meals that we learned how to talk to strangers, listen to grown-up conversations, report on the Sunday school lesson or our impression of the sermon, and sit still until it was time to clear the table.

After dinner, my father read from the big, white Bible storybook with the puffy, gold-embossed cover, colorful pictures inside, and hymns printed in the back matter. Incidentally, it is the same Bible storybook that Audrey and Emma discovered this past Christmas at Gran and Papa's house. The same Bible storybook they listened to Papa read from every night of their visit, before falling asleep under a patchwork quilt made by my great-grandmother.

As we grew up, we read different books. And when we could read well enough, we took turns reading from our Bibles—Ephesians, Galatians, 1 John. By the time we reached high school, it was *Morning and Evening* by Charles Spurgeon.

After we had read, prayed, and occasionally sung at least one verse of "The Old Rugged Cross" (one of my favorite hymns to this day), Kristen and I would wash and dry the dishes. I remember that we were glad when it was our night to wash, because whoever dried the dishes also had to put them away.

Dinner with Jesus

Jesus, too, must have a lot of mealtime memories from His time here on earth. The Gospels are full of stories of His eating.

He often used mealtime as time to teach. It was at a meal that he said, "A new command I give you: Love one another. As I have loved you, so you must love one another" (John 13:34). From the dinner table, He assures us of the many rooms in His Father's house and promises the coming of the Holy Spirit.

His very first miracle, in fact, took place at a wedding feast. The host (or hostess, I suppose) hadn't planned well and ran out of wine. What panic she must have felt. It's not like there was a grocery store around the corner where she could send a servant to replenish the supply.

Even with a grocery store around the corner, I have a crazy fear about running out of food when we have company. I think I get it from my mother. Toben laughs at me when I begin cooking for a party. He's always looking around for more people to invite when he sees the amount of food I make.

Jesus must have understood this, because He turned some water into wine and saved the party—along with the hostess's reputation. Not surprisingly, the wine He provided was even better than what the host first served (John 2:1–11).

The disciples understood the importance of having enough food, I think. When the crowds, multitudes, masses of people who'd come to hear Jesus teach got hungry, the disciples panicked. "You've got to send them away—now, before they get any hungrier! We don't have enough food!" Instead of complying with their request, Jesus turned to them and said, "You give them something to eat" (see Mark 6). I'm sure the disciples thought He was crazy. Now, children might have gone along with a pretend tea party; but I'm pretty sure the adults wouldn't have been satisfied with mud pies and imaginary tea.

Ironic, then, that it was a child who gladly offered his meager lunch to feed the crowd—as if he were certain that if the disciples just used their imaginations, it would be enough. And of course it was—with leftovers.

Wouldn't it have been fun to see and share in that meal? Food always tastes better on a picnic. And let's remember, the food wasn't fancy; rather, it was made from what was available. When you're hungry and all together, it's the sharing of a meal that's most important—not whether the fish is sautéed, broiled, or grilled.

Jesus must have known how good food tastes when you're hungry and tired from working hard. He probably put Himself in the disciples' shoes, to know exactly what would be perfect when He cooked them breakfast on the shore of Galilee.

Imagine coming in from a long night of fishing on the lake. Dawn is breaking and your fingers are stiff and cold from hauling nets up into the boat and lowering them down into the water—again and again through the night. Your arms are aching, your back is aching, your toes are cold from the little bit of water that's always standing in the bottom of the boat.

As you pull your boat up onto the sand, you smell wood smoke and look up to see a fire crackling in the early morning light. A friend—your Friend—beckons you to come and warm your hands by the fire. Your fingers tingle as the feeling returns to your hands; your stomach growls from the tantalizing smell of roasting fish. Oh, to sit with your feet toward the fire as you eat a hot breakfast—would anything taste so good? Would anything feel so wonderful?

How amazing it is to think that Jesus knows just what we need when we need it!

Of course, Jesus ate at home, too—at the homes of Zacchaeus and of Mary and Martha, for example. In fact, the first thing He did upon meeting Zacchaeus was to invite Himself over for dinner. Jesus seemed to know that mealtimes provide the perfect opportunity to get to know others. It's easy to relax over a meal—you can look at people's faces, talk about your day, your week, your life.

At our dinner table, Audrey usually asks each of us the same question: "What was the best part of your day?" Our answers always vary—from sitting down together for a meal, to seeing a dolphin at the beach, to spending time with a friend. But whatever the answer, all it takes is a follow-up question, "Why?"—and you have instant conversation.

Food and Fellowship

It shouldn't be too surprising that so much of what we read about Jesus occurs at mealtime. God has always put value on such fellowship.

While the practice of sacrifice in the Old Testament isn't very appealing to me, my friend Bill pointed me in a direction that caused me to think about it a little bit differently. (I have to wonder what would happen if the temple in Jerusalem were rebuilt and sacrifices were made again. Would the world allow it? All those poor animals slaughtered and burned.)

Here's the thought...sacrifice was really a meal shared with God in a strange sort of way. God describes sacrifices as a sweet fragrance and a pleasing aroma; He took delight in the scent of a meal offered up to him.

Maybe my delight in coming home from church to a house that smells of pot roast is a reflection of being made in God's image.

Especially when we look at the fellowship offering. We see

clearly that God wants to dine with us—to share a time of communion and fellowship. The fellowship offering was a voluntary offering, a time of fellowship with God that included a communal meal. It was the only sacrifice in which the one offering the sacrifice took part in eating it. In this meal, meat, wine, bread, and oil were offered in balanced proportion. Roasted meat, bread dipped in oil, a glass of red wine. Sounds like a pretty good meal, doesn't it?

The fact that God wants to eat with us shouldn't be surprising. After all, we quote Revelation 3:20 often: "Here I am! I stand at the door and knock. If anyone hears my voice and opens the door, I will come in."

But look at the rest of the verse: "*I will come in and eat with him, and he with me.*" God values eating together!

Just think about all of the things in Scripture that pertain to eating communally—the Passover meal, Communion, and even the early church ate meals together—the birth of the church potluck, if you will! And the beginning of eternity in heaven is going to be celebrated with a meal we'll share with all the saints and God Himself—the marriage supper of the Lamb (Revelation 19:9). I can hardly wait.

Meals Are More than Food

I've said before that I love the story about Mary and Martha having Jesus over to dine in their home. I can so totally relate to Martha, who rushed about trying to have the meal come out just right. It's difficult enough today, juggling ovens and multiple burners, to get the bread, potatoes, green beans, and turkey to finish cooking at the same time. Imagine how Martha felt. No dishwasher, no canned cranberry sauce, no timer on her stove. No wonder she was stressed out.

I often have to stop—especially when company's coming—and remind myself that there's more to the meal than what we're eating. The point of mealtime is to be together, to learn about each other, to grow together. Mealtime should be a time of enjoying one another's company. As I struggle to remind myself, it's not about the food—no matter how hard I may have worked to prepare it.

As the Book of Wisdom so wisely states: "Better a meal of vegetables where there is love than a fattened calf with hatred" (Proverbs 15:17); and "Better a dry crust with peace and quiet than a house full of feasting, with strife" (Proverbs 17:1).

There's that attitude thing again!

What is mealtime like at your house? Are you more worried about what's on the table than what's going on around it? Is mealtime what you want it to be? If not, what needs to be added or changed?

We have a great opportunity, through mealtime, to serve our families and others, to teach our children to enjoy being together, and so much more.

Learning to Pray

Along with bedtime, mealtime is a time for teaching my children to pray. It's an obvious place to pause and give thanks for the food on the table.

My children love to sing their prayers. Here are our favorites for mealtimes:

Oh, the Lord's been good to me!
And so I thank the Lord
For giving me the things I need:
The sun and the moon and the appleseed.
The Lord is good to me!
Amen. Amen. Amen. Amen. Amen! Amen!
(sung to the tune of "Johnny Appleseed")

We always add in that extra little "amen"—it makes our company smile even as they wonder whether it will ever end. (Emma opens her mouth so wide to sing her "amen's"—I usually find myself laughing at her instead of getting that final "amen" in!)

Another favorite is this one:

God, our Father,
God, our Father,
We thank you,
We thank you.
For our many blessings,
For our many blessings.
Amen. Amen.
(sung to the tune of "Frère Jacques")

This one can be sung in a round, which is Audrey's and Emma's favorite way to sing it when we have company and lots of people around the table—girls first, then boys. They love to finish their part first and listen to the boys complete the "amen's." They also like to sing it in a round when it's just the four of us (Audrey waits to start, but usually ends up singing along with the people who went first, and then just adding some extra "amen's" at the end).

This last is one my family learned when we lived in England, while I was in junior high school. We always sang it with the Hemsleys, a family that adopted us as part of their family. It is sung to the tune of "Edelweiss" (from *The Sound of Music*):

Bless our friends, bless our food.
Come, O Lord, and sit with us.
May our hearts glow with peace,
May Your love surround us.

Friendship and love, may they bloom and grow,
Bloom and grow forever.
Bless our friends, bless our food.
Come, O Lord, and sit with us.

Thinking about it puts me right back in their dining room, holding hands around a table laden with food. I remember the smell of roast beef filling the room and the sweet sound of Eva's voice, thick with a Yorkshire accent, as we stood behind our chairs, mouths watering.

At our house, we take turns praying at dinner every night. Audrey usually speaks her prayers and wants to hold hands. Emma prefers to sing and requests that everyone hold their hands together, palms flat against each other, as we pray.

Manners, Please!

Family mealtime provides the perfect setting in which to teach our children the value of manners. Who among us hasn't heard, at one point or another, "Mind your manners!"? Or, for that matter, said it to our own children?

It was at home around the dinner table that I learned to chew with my mouth closed, to keep my elbows off the table, to place my napkin in my lap, to pass the salt and pepper together. It was at home that I learned about cutlery—that the fork goes on the left, where to place the dessert spoon, and, when in doubt about which utensil was appropriate, that I should start at the outside and work my way in.

When we teach our children manners and etiquette at home, we equip them with the confidence and knowledge they will need to go new places and face new things.

Mealtime is also a great time to entertain. As Lucy Maud Montgomery wrote, "Where can folks get better acquainted than over a meal table?"[37]

I recently read an article in a 1937 issue of *Better Homes and Gardens*. Titled "Company Once a Week," the article encouraged readers to invite others into their homes for dinner. Take a look:

> In fact, the more we keep up our weekly entertaining, the more I see in it besides the fun of the thing. It's really doing things to us as a family. We're closer knit, more interested in each other, less inclined to think of home merely as a roosting place between mad dashes here and there. The children are more natural and also more courteous and easy in the presence of outsiders. And I (pardon my rank immodesty) am turning into no mean hostess.[38]

A while back we invited another family over for dinner. We lit the fire pit in the backyard, roasted hot dogs, and ate baked beans. For dessert, we made s'mores. We also filled bananas with chocolate chips and miniature marshmallows, wrapped them in foil, and cooked them in the hot coals. Gourmet it was not. But oh, what fun!

That's why I smiled when I read in the *Better Homes and Gardens* article, "Just a simple supper winding up with an old-fashioned sing, yet it was one grand time from start to finish!"[39]

After eating our s'mores and roasted bananas, we sat around the fire and sang every song we could remember from all the summer camps we went to as kids. We had a grand time, and I hope the kids will remember it always. I loved it.

Even if the company you invite for dinner doesn't include other children, your children can still benefit. They will learn to listen to conversation, to ask questions politely, to talk to adults they don't really know.

$$\infty$$

Back to the *Betsy-Tacy* books. (If you haven't read them, I can't recommend them enough. They are delightful!) While she struggled to learn to cook, Betsy's friend Tacy offered lots of helpful advice—especially about entertaining.

> "Hello!" Tacy called from the kitchen. She was kneeling at the oven, gingerly drawing out a roasting pan. She lifted it to the top of the stove, and transferred a plump, savory bird to a hot platter.
>
> "Roast chicken," she remarked, covering it snugly, "and chocolate meringue pie are my company dinner. It's a great help, Betsy, to have one company dinner that you know how to make really well."[40]

Do you have a "company dinner"—a menu that you've perfected over time? If not, think about something you make really well, something you can put together with relative ease; then make *that* your company dinner.

I'd have to go with Tacy and say that roast chicken is one of my best company dinners, too. I love the fact that nearly all the preparation can be done in advance, so there's no last-minute rushing around. It makes the house smell so good, and by adding a green salad, steamed vegetables, and a great dessert, you end up with an elegant meal.

Plus, roasting chickens are not expensive, and the leftovers can be turned into homemade chicken noodle soup!

I learned to make roast chicken from Pierrette, my French professor in college. Her apartment, located on the South Hill in Spokane, had huge picture windows overlooking the city. The walls were covered in artwork—framed prints, original paintings, photographs. She would give Toben and me the key to her apartment, and we'd let ourselves in after stopping at the grocery store. By the time she arrived with our favorite English professor in tow, the house smelled wonderful!

Here's the full menu (I've modified it a bit over the years), followed by recipes:

Baked Brie

Scarborough Chicken

Green Salad

"Joanne" Carrots

Chocolate Mousse

Baked Brie

This is soooo good—and easy! In fact, it is one of those recipes that tastes way more complicated than it is. The melted Brie mixes with the brown sugar, the pecans are toasted and crunchy, and every bite tastes like heaven. Everyone will ask you for the recipe.

Place a round of Brie in an ovenproof dish (the one you'll serve it in). Mix together 1 cup chopped pecans and ½ cup brown sugar; sprinkle evenly over the Brie. Bake in a 350°F oven until the cheese runs when pierced with a knife, about 25 minutes. Serve accompanied by sliced apples, sliced pears, and French bread or crackers.

Scarborough Chicken

Remove the giblets from a fairly large roasting chicken, then rinse and pat dry; place in a shallow roasting pan. Juice a lemon through a sieve and sprinkle the lemon juice in the cavity. Rub the chicken all over with olive oil and then sprinkle liberally with a mixture of minced garlic, kosher salt, and pepper. Finally, add a generous sprinkling of either fresh or dried herbs—equal parts parsley, sage, rosemary, and thyme. (Just think of the song lyrics: "Are you going to Scarborough Fair? Parsley, sage, rosemary, and thyme.")

Pour about 2 cups of vermouth into the pan and roast in a 350°F oven for about 1 hour and 20 minutes, or until juices run clear. Baste from time to time with the pan juices. If the skin begins to brown early, tent with foil; remove during the last 10 minutes of roasting.

Serve the chicken on a platter, surrounded with rosemary springs, and carve tableside. Or, if you're uncertain about your carving skills, cut it up in the kitchen just before serving, and then transfer the pieces to a platter.

An elegant presentation tip: Thinly slice the juiced lemon and stuff the slices, along with whole sage leaves, under the chicken's skin before roasting.

Green Salad

I like romaine lettuce paired with a simple homemade vinaigrette. To make your own dressing, combine 1 part vinegar (any kind) with 2 parts olive oil; add 1 teaspoon Dijon mustard, 1 teaspoon sugar, a few grindings of salt and pepper, and tarragon to taste; mix thoroughly. (I usually combine the ingredients in a jelly jar and shake it until emulsified.) Toss lightly with salad greens just before serving.

"Joanne" Carrots

These should really be called "Pierrette" carrots, since she taught me to make them. But I've prepared them so often myself that my aunt began calling them "Joanne" carrots...and the name stuck.

Steam baby carrots until tender. In a small saucepan, toss the steamed carrots with butter until coated. Sprinkle with chopped garlic to taste (I like mine garlicky), salt, and about 1/4 cup of sugar. The sweet-salty combination of the sugar, butter, and garlic is what makes these so good! Add a generous sprinkling of fresh chopped parsley and serve hot.

Chocolate Mousse

I got this recipe from Pierrette as well. It's very simple to make.

Combine 1/3 cup very hot coffee with one 12-ounce package of semisweet chocolate chips in the top of a double boiler (or, alternatively, a metal bowl placed over a pan of boiling water). Stir constantly until the chocolate is melted and the mixture is smooth. Remove from heat and beat in 4 egg yolks. Let cool slightly.

In a separate bowl, beat 4 egg whites until stiff. Pour the cooled chocolate mixture over the egg whites and fold together gently until no streaks of white remain. Transfer to a glass bowl or spoon into individual serving cups—porcelain ramekins or wine glasses work well— and chill for at least an hour.

Just before serving, garnish each dessert with a dollop of whipped cream, some chopped toasted pecans, and shaved chocolate or chocolate-covered coffee beans.

Of course, once you begin inviting the same people over for dinner, you may need to come up with another menu!

The bottom line is, family dinner doesn't have to be complicated. Start small, start simple, and go from there. If your family never eats dinner together, pick one night a week to begin. Making family dinner a priority may involve modifying your schedules and reprioritizing commitments. You may have to work to get your family on board.

Take a poll on what everyone wants for dinner. Make it fun by getting your children involved with the meal preparation. Make dinnertime a family affair.

And don't forget—there are other meals to share, too. Breakfasts before school, lazy Saturday morning brunches, Sunday dinners following church. There are so many opportunities to make mealtime special for your family. Pick one and get started!

I love to tell the story, for those who know it best
Seem hungering and thirsting to hear it like the rest.
And when, in scenes of glory, I sing the new, new song,
'Twill be the old, old story that I have loved so long.[41]

Simple Celebrations

I LOVE THE IDEA OF THE UNBIRTHDAY PARTY FROM *Alice in Wonderland.* Who hasn't woken up on a beautiful day and wished for an Unbirthday Party? For that matter, why do we seem to outgrow birthday parties as we grow older? Sure, the "biggies" still get celebrated, but what about 24 and 32 and 47 and 56?

I love celebrations. Since we're talking about birthdays here, I have to acknowledge that I've been a little intimidated by birthday parties since moving to Southern California. You wouldn't believe some of the parties my kids have been invited to. This is the land of MTV's *My Super Sweet Sixteen,* after all, and parents of elementary-school kids are practicing years in advance. Bounce houses, cotton candy machines, country clubs...you name it and it's what's happening for six-year-olds. Dozens of children, even more presents. I find myself wondering, *Where will they put all the stuff they get?*

With all that, I wasn't quite sure whether to believe Audrey when she told me a friend would celebrate her seventh birthday by taking some friends to New York to stay in a hotel and visit the American Girl store. "We're going to fly on a plane and stay in a hotel with a swimming pool and go shopping and get new dolls," she said. "Can I go? Please?"

"Hmmm," I said. Turns out the grandiose details were mere wishful thinking on her friend's part, and I didn't have to make the decision. But for a few days there, I wasn't sure how to respond to something so incredible—especially when Audrey came home each day with a list of all the other girls who were going!

To be honest, I'm just plain afraid to throw a party for my kids here. So far I've stuck to the "birthdays are for families" rule. It's working—but then, my kids are still young.

And since they are young, I'm doing my darnedest to scale back on celebrations now. I just had the conversation with my mother about simplifying Christmas this year. Now, my mother is the queen of Christmas. She won't necessarily take apart a pack of gum and wrap each stick individually...but close!

She said they tried to simplify Christmas once when my sister and I were little—three gifts each (one for each of the wise men, they told us) and a birthday cake for Jesus. "It was the worst Christmas ever," she said. After years of opening gifts slowly and stopping every so often for snacks, she said, the whole thing was over before it really began. In fact, she added, it felt like the Thanksgiving dinner you spend hours preparing that everyone gobbles down in about ten minutes flat!

The funny thing is that I don't remember it at all, so I'm willing to give it a shot for my kids. And because Christmas is more fun when it lasts all day, I guess I'll have to come up with some fun activities to fill up the time. We'll see how it turns out.

Birthdays, anniversaries, Christmas, Easter, Thanksgiving... Opportunities to celebrate happen often in our lives. We look forward to them with mixed emotions—Christmas is fun, but comes with a huge to-do list and a bigger bill. And after everything is opened, you have to find a place to put it all!

Easter has been reduced to bunny rabbits and jelly beans...a mad race to see who finds the most plastic eggs and ends up with the most cavities two months down the road. New dresses and how we look in our Easter bonnets take precedence over the real reason for Easter.

Thanksgiving requires using every pot you own and juggling burners and oven space to somehow have everything cooked at the same time so it all arrives on the table hot and in the right order. What do I end up most thankful for? That I get to sit down—finally!—after slaving in the kitchen for six hours straight.

Of course I'm exaggerating a bit, but you get the picture. And I'm guessing you can relate...at least a little. It seems like we save up all of our celebration hopes and dreams for the "biggies." And then when we get bogged down in all of the trappings, we end up disappointed. After all that anticipation and work, it's over in fifteen minutes.

We've lost much of the joy in celebrating together and have traded the pleasure of simply being together for more and more consumption. We talk about simplifying and saying, "Enough!" We want it, we dream about it...but we're not sure how our kids will react. How do we stand firm when our extended families, neighbors, friends, and our children's friends expect bigger and better each year?

What would happen if we simplified our celebrations—not by banning Christmas presents or burning our Easter baskets, but by bringing celebration into the everyday-ness of our lives?

What would happen if we stopped to ask ourselves what it is we're celebrating and focused on that rather than the stuff? What would happen if we created traditions and routines around the things that really matter?

☙

What does it mean to celebrate, anyway? The dictionary says that the verb *celebrate* means "to do something to show that a day or event is important, to honor with festivities, to make merry on such an occasion."[42]

Here's how I look at it: Every day is important, *festivity* is a great word, and there are many things to be merry about.

So how do we do that?

I recently read *The House at Pooh Corner* by A. A. Milne. I couldn't recall reading it before, and I was surprised at how many times I laughed, how often I read a line or two aloud to whoever was nearby. If you haven't read it in a while—or ever—go get a copy.

I think Pooh understood celebrating the everyday. In one scene, Piglet and Pooh are getting ready to visit everyone. Piglet suddenly decides they must have a reason to call on all their friends (other than hoping for an invitation to tea and a "little smackerel of something").

Pooh comes up with a *great* reason. "We'll go because it's Thursday," he tells Piglet, "and we'll go to wish everybody a Very Happy Thursday."

Sometimes, you have to get creative.

Happy "I Love You" Day

I don't remember exactly when "Happy I Love You" Day began, but I think it was in college and involved a Slurpee.

I love Slurpees, and Toben knows how much I love them. One hot day he surprised me at work with a peach Slurpee—the hardest flavor to find, and also, I think, the best.

And so "Happy I Love You" Day was born.

The great thing about this celebration is that it happens whenever you want. The other great thing is that it's always a surprise. And I love surprises!

Through the years of our marriage, "Happy I Love You" Day has been celebrated in big ways (a surprise trip to Carmel for the whole family) and small ways (a box of Good & Plenty). Mostly, it involves putting yourself in the other person's place and thinking of something that would make him or her happy.

The things we do for "Happy I Love You" Day are generally pretty ordinary; they're things you've probably done yourself at one time or another. The difference is that in our family, we've given it a name and turned it into a tradition.

Go ahead, start "Happy I Love You" Day in your family. I'm glad for you to borrow the idea and make it your own. Or find something else that your family likes to do and turn it into something special. Ice Cream Friday. Monday Night Spaghetti. (I must be hungry—all of these seem to be about food!)

It could be as simple as taking a walk each night after dinner, or reading the same book at bedtime. Playing cards on a Friday night or watching cartoons together on Saturday morning. It doesn't have to be something big or expensive or elaborate. You can take just about anything and make it special and fun—it becomes special because it's something *your* family does together.

❧

I want to take the time to celebrate the small things about daily life—a good grade Audrey received on her spelling test, a beautiful Saturday morning, Emma learning to write her name, Toben's "best ride ever" while surfing.

So how do I do this? With the girls, I think it's sometimes as simple as putting down whatever I'm working on and giving them my full attention while they describe in detail their latest accomplishment or victory. By looking Audrey in the eye and listening, I convey that I'm really proud of her and that I celebrate her achievement. By putting down the dish towel and asking Toben to tell me what made this wave better than all the others he's ridden, I give him the opportunity to celebrate surfing.

Celebrate the Story

But some celebrations require more than just listening. Some celebrations are more complex and take more time.

Christmas, Thanksgiving, Easter, birthdays, anniversaries. How do we celebrate these kinds of things and see past the wrapping paper and ribbon, the candy and cake?

By celebrating the story, not the stuff.

This epiphany just hit me—while I was brushing my teeth, of all things. It's such a simple idea. I can't believe it hasn't struck me before.

We ran to the store this morning to pick up some supplies for an Easter craft. Easter is still a month away, but when we woke up on this Saturday morning it was raining, and I knew that if I didn't come up with something fun, engaging, and most of all *messy* for the girls to do, they'd choose to spend the entire day in front of the television. So off to the store we went, in search of small wooden crates to decorate as treasure boxes.

We decorated for Easter last week, getting out all the little bunnies and baskets, chicks and bird nests. We tucked little surprises here and there to find, and we got out the Easter books.

Our collection of Easter books isn't very large. In fact, there are only three. But one of them is a book we love so much that we haven't felt like we really need more. We read *Benjamin's Box* over and over—both out loud and individually. Audrey will read it to Emma, and Emma will "read" it to herself, following the pictures to know what part of the story to tell.

It's the story of a little boy named Benjamin, who has a treasure box given to him by his grandfather. There's nothing in the box when the story begins, save for a few pieces of straw that came from the bed of a baby boy who was said to be a king. Benjamin is not sure about it, but he's got his eyes open for treasures to store in his special box.

He hears about Jesus and follows Him from the time He enters Jerusalem on a donkey. Eventually, Benjamin finds a silver coin, a bit of gauze, a thorn. And on Easter morning, he discovers an empty tomb and a piece of stone broken off from the large stone that was rolled away.

At the end of the book, Benjamin's box is full. He shares with his friends about each item in the box, about the treasure it represents. He passes the items around so they can touch and hold and discover their shape and feel.

"And so you see," he says as he closes the box and looks into their faces, "*the treasure is really Jesus.* Because of what Jesus did on the cross, we can all be forgiven by God the Father!"

And the children cheer and beg him to tell the story again.[43]

Can't you hear it? Children pleading, "Tell us the story again!" (It reminds me of how my mother indulged my sister's request to read *Best Nest* so often that Kristen thought she could read because she knew every word by heart.)

So Audrey, Emma, and I ripped up bits of tissue paper, dipped paintbrushes in glue, and decoupaged to our hearts' content. Their boxes are drying, and each box already holds a piece of gauze from the medicine cabinet, three silver coins, and a die—just a few of the items they'll collect to remind them of the parts of the Easter story.

The girls have the complete list of things they need lodged firmly in their minds, and they'll be on the lookout to collect them by the time Easter comes around. They'll search for a thorn to remind them of Jesus' crown of thorns, a stone to represent the one rolled away from the tomb, a scrap of purple cloth for the robe the soldiers put on Jesus. *Benjamin's Box* talks about each item they can collect, and they've already thought of others to add, making their boxes unique to them. On Easter morning, they'll remove each item, one by one, and tell the story of Easter.

And Toben and I will cheer and beg them to tell the story again.

Tell Me a Story

The Bible is full of stories.

In the Old Testament, Genesis tells the story of creation, the stories of Abraham, Isaac, and Jacob. Exodus tells the story of plagues, miracles, and Moses. The books of Samuel and the books of Kings tell the story of kings and battles, friendships and betrayals. The book of Esther tells the story of an ordinary girl who becomes a queen and saves her people. Daniel tells the story of lions and fiery furnaces.

In the New Testament, the Gospels tell the story of God incarnate—Jesus, God's own Son, who loved to tell stories. Take a look at this verse from Matthew: "All Jesus did that day was tell stories—a long storytelling afternoon" (13:34, *The Message*).

The Gospels are also full of parables, stories of everyday life that Jesus used to teach a lesson or make a point. He told stories and asked His listeners to interact with those stories. "Tell me what you think of this story," Jesus began (Matthew 21:28, *The Message*).

The book of Acts tells stories about men struck blind, shipwrecks, jailbreaks, and healing. I remember Beth Moore saying that the Bible is full of stories that would capture the imagination of any child—stories that beat any storybook ever written.

Clearly, God loves to tell stories.

And children love to listen to stories. Maybe that's one of the things Jesus meant when He said we must become like little children in order to enter the kingdom—perhaps He meant that we must love to listen to stories.

"Tell me a story!" It's something we've all said and heard.

"Read me a story!" my children plead before bedtime.

Unfortunately, at some point, we seem to think we've outgrown stories. (Sure, we read *fiction*, but not *stories*.) We associate stories with childhood, with the unreal, the imaginary. We read Scripture as mere history and closely and carefully examine its details for theological impact; we neglect to lose ourselves in the story of God wanting us so much that He sent His own Son to earth as a baby, His own Son "who did not consider equality with God something to be grasped, but made himself nothing" as Paul so beautifully wrote in Philippians 2:6–7.

As a child, I remember being fascinated by *The Neverending Story*. Such a wonderful thought—a story that never ends but goes on and on and on. I hate coming to the end of a book I love. I purposely pick out huge novels when I visit the library—the thicker the better—because I want to delay that slowing down, that feeling of dread when the pages left to be read are fewer than the ones I've already read.

Maybe that, too, is part of being created for eternity in the image of an eternal God. We long to be part of a story that never ends.

Though we are created for eternity, our stories do have a beginning—and we remember that beginning each year when our birthdays come around.

Let's celebrate the story of birth, of our beginnings.

Remember the scene in *City Slickers* when Billy Crystal's character wakes up to the phone ringing on his birthday? His mother has called to tell him the story of his birth. He rolls his eyes and mouths the words along with her, for he knows the story by heart; he hears her tell it every year.

We laugh as he hangs up and complains to his wife, but there's something wonderful in his mother's insistence on telling him the story every year.

What's the story of your birth? Your child's birth?

My sister recently visited with her baby, and I pulled out Audrey's and Emma's baby books to remember when they first crawled and when their first tooth arrived. "I want to see!" they said. "Read it to me!"

Birthdays are a chance to tell our children their stories. Tell the story again and again—children love to hear the stories of their lives, to fill in details we omit. "You forgot the part about..." they say.

When did you find out you were pregnant, or get a call telling you a child was yours? How did you tell people your news? Were there showers? What did you feel when you first held your child in your arms? What were your hopes, dreams, fears? What do you remember about your child? What cute things did your child do or say?

What are your own favorite birthday memories? Talk about your birthday traditions or birthday stories from your family. Create some new traditions. Get out family movies and photo albums. Take pictures to look back on in years to come.

Birthdays are an opportunity to celebrate the stories of our births, our lives. They are a chance to evaluate, to celebrate. How have we changed in the past year? How have we grown? What are our hopes for the upcoming year?

Do we see progress in our children? Are they ready for new

responsibilities, new privileges? Is it time to add an allowance, time to extend their bedtime?

Do we see progress and growth in ourselves, our friends, our family? How have we seen faith grow and develop in the past year? Tell the story!

By focusing primarily on the presents and party, we sell ourselves short. We settle for the temporary—the toys and other gifts that will inevitably break or get lost or be forgotten—when the story is waiting to be told and a new chapter is waiting to be written.

I remember a few birthday parties growing up, but what I mostly remember is just being with my family. Getting to choose my birthday dinner (grilled flank steak and sautéed mushrooms was a favorite for a while, followed closely by fondue), the kind of dessert I wanted (anything chocolate!), and a few gifts from my parents. Despite the lack of pomp and circumstance, birthdays always felt different and special. Birthdays were just for family.

I look back on the birthdays we've celebrated and am a little saddened about all the opportunities we've missed to celebrate the story. There was the birthday for Emma when the cake didn't—wouldn't!—turn out right and I ended up throwing the whole thing in the trash and starting from scratch the morning of the party. Talk about a stressed-out mom on the edge! Or the hours spent planning a fairy party for Audrey that didn't come to pass because we ended up being out of town for her birthday.

Wouldn't it be wonderful to stop stressing over parties and cakes and frosting and presents, and instead focus on celebrating the person? Instead of wandering through Target looking for something—*anything*—to wrap up for your child, what if you put the time and thought and care and effort into celebrating his or her life story?

Make a scrapbook each year that chronicles all that's happened since the last birthday. Write the book of the birthday person's life by adding a new chapter each year. Create an ongoing collage of photos, movie ticket stubs, or artwork, and then make a gift of it. Compose a poem to celebrate the past year, or write out a blessing over the year to come.

Celebrating the story of birth has infinite possibilities.

The Christmas Story

The story of Christmas is the greatest birth story ever told. God incarnate, come to earth to save us in the form of a tiny baby. A scared and unmarried girl, pregnant by one not her betrothed. A king, fearful and vengeful enough to murder innocent children. Shepherds, minding their sheep and witness to the heavenly host singing "Gloria." Wise men, bearing costly and strangely impractical gifts for a baby king.

I grew up in the church and have always been familiar with the Christmas story. It was read aloud each Christmas and became part of the celebration, just like the tree and presents and carols. The story was the reason for it all, but the story didn't really stand out above anything else. That is, it didn't grab hold of me then the way it does now.

As an adult, my imagination runs a little wild when I think of Mary sitting down to tell her parents that she was with child. I imagine the relief Mary must have felt when her cousin Elizabeth believed her story. My heart breaks for the mothers of Bethlehem, mourning their baby boys killed only because they were born too soon or too late to escape Herod's fear. I wonder about the innkeeper and his family, about Mary's parents and Joseph's friends and all the other people who must have been so affected by this story we tell each year. How do we celebrate the story of Christmas more than the stuff of Christmas?

To begin, we have to tell the story. "Do you remember?" is how some of my favorite conversations begin.

"Do you remember the story of Christmas?" we ask one another as we set out the crèche, putting each piece in place.

"This is the shepherd," Emma says as she puts him in place.

"Don't forget his sheep," Audrey reminds her as she places the pewter lamb next to the manger, and then hands Emma a cow.

They add wise men and camels, Mary and Joseph. They work hard to balance the angel above the stable—the angel whose banner reads, "Gloria."

We celebrated Advent this past Christmas, lighting candles on the Sundays preceding Christmas, talking about what each candle means and reminding ourselves of the parts of the story that led to Jesus' birth.

Advent was something we celebrated from time to time when I was a child. We lit candles at church and Sunday dinner. But Advent as a season of waiting, of preparing for Jesus to be born, is something I'm still pursuing.

As with pregnancy, the season of Advent culminates in the birth of a child—the Christ child. We grow heavy as the waiting becomes more and more difficult. *Is it time yet?* we wonder. "How many more days?" we ask. Just when we think we can't wait another day, Christmas arrives—and a new chapter in our own story is written.

The Advent guide we followed included a wonderful idea to add new parts of the crèche each week: You have the shepherds show up one week, the Magi another, and finally the baby in the manger on Christmas morning. I thought about following it, but the girls would rather play with the pewter figures all together—move them around, have them interact with each other and make conversation.

I like how they see the pieces of the crèche: as objects in a story, just waiting for their imagination to make them come alive.

☙

Like the Easter boxes, the crèche helps us celebrate the story of Christmas.

Mary, too, appreciated the things that make up the story of the Incarnation. "But Mary treasured up all these things and pondered them in her heart" (Luke 2:19).

I noticed heart-shaped boxes at the store when we bought our Easter boxes. What treasures do you suppose Mary might have stored in her heart?

Perhaps she kept a piece of straw, a scrap of the swaddling clothes, a slip of paper with their family tree, linking them to "the house and lineage of David." Maybe she kept a lock of hair, baby soft and curled at the end, a baby tooth, a curl of wood from her son's first carpentry project. Perhaps she kept a piece of the gold, a small amount of frankincense and myrrh. Maybe she kept a soft bit of fleece from the shepherds who came to visit; perhaps she wrote down the words of Simeon or Anna.

So many possibilities. So many things we can use to remind us of the story of Christmas. Something tells me we'll be collecting treasures for new boxes when Christmas comes. It will be fun to see how our treasure boxes turn out!

Your Christmas Story

We tell our own stories of Christmas alongside God's story of Christmas. How has Christ been born in each of us? When did we make room for Him in our full and busy lives?

Along with the gifts we give to friends and family, what will we give to the Christ child this Christmas?

What are the stories of our Christmases past? What traditions do we have? Tell their stories and talk about where they came from. Share special recipes, laugh over memories, and tell the stories that make your family your own.

Gift your family with a blessing, create a time capsule or a letter to read next Christmas, get out your family photos and create an album for the year that's coming to a close. Talk about your memories of the year and tell the stories that stand out to you.

My sister is a professional photographer and often gives us photographs for Christmas. "I know it's not much," she often says, perhaps because it comes so easily to her or doesn't cost as much as other gifts. But these gifts from her are our favorite to receive.

There's the picture of Audrey and Emma at the beach. Wearing bright pink and purple wetsuits, they stand together, with Emma's head tucked close under Audrey's arm, and Audrey leaning over so her head rests on top of Emma's.

Or the photograph of the girls and me in bed on a family vacation in Estes Park. I'm lying between the girls, and they are tucked in close—one under each arm. My eyes are closed, but Audrey and Emma are looking directly at the camera.

There are the architectural photographs of Paris—the Eiffel Tower, Notre Dame, the steps leading up to Montmartre. All reminding me of the summer Toben and I lived in Paris, exploring new corners of the city each weekend.

How can you celebrate your family's story this Christmas?

The Passover Story

We celebrated Passover this year for the first time. Each plate was set with a taste of horseradish, the *haroset* mixture of apples and nuts and honey, a sprig of parsley, a bowl of saltwater, broken pieces of matzo, four glasses of grape juice. I think God understands that we learn best when we can hold and touch and taste what He wants us to know.

Each place setting included a Passover *Haggadah*—a booklet that outlined the steps in the meal, walking us through what to say and when. The children all tasted the salty water on the parsley and understood that it represented the tears cried by the Jews when they were enslaved in Egypt. They wrinkled their noses when they tasted the bitter horseradish, making the connection with the bitterness of slavery. And they tasted the horseradish again—this time with a bite of *haroset*, noting that the sweetness of Jesus' love makes the bitterness recede.

They listened carefully while we talked about each cup of juice. We drank gladly from the Cup of Sanctification, the cup that sets us apart as God's own people. They saw the Cup of Judgment go untouched—because Jesus drank it willingly for us. Then we drank from the Cup of Redemption, grateful that Jesus paid the price for our sin. We left the final cup—the Cup of the Kingdom—untouched also, because we will wait to drink it in heaven with Jesus.

They understood it so well that when someone accidentally reached for his second cup, they yelled, "Don't drink that one, you'll die!" We laughed at their reaction, glad to see the meaning had made its impression.

And it wasn't just the children who learned from the meal. As adults, we too saw how completely Jesus became our Passover lamb, how perfectly He met the requirements, how completely God saw to each detail of the final sacrifice for our sin.

Sharing a Passover meal lent new significance to the sacrifice Jesus made, new joy and enthusiasm as we greeted one another on Easter Sunday with the cry, "He is risen! He is risen indeed!"

What else can we celebrate? What stories are part of your family? Here are some ideas:

> The first day of school and all the first days that have gone before.
>
> Your anniversary and the story of your relationship. Tell your children, show them pictures, watch the movie. Tell them the story until they "remember" when you met for the first time and can recall the details as if they too had been there.
>
> Thanksgiving and the different ways you've demonstrated your thankfulness each year.
>
> The first day of spring.

It doesn't have to be anything big—you can pick something and start a new story. My aunt and cousin used to miss school and head up to San Juan Capistrano each spring to see the swallows as they returned. They would pack orange juice and muffins to eat on the train, and off they would go every year.

One friend turns just about everything at her house green each year for St. Patrick's Day. Milk, the kids' lunches, even the water in the toilet. "Leprechauns" come and turn chairs upside down and leave funny gifts.

Another family plants flowers together on the first day of spring. They dig in the dirt, open seed packets, and water carefully.

Growing up, we watched the Rose Parade on television every New Year's Day and wrote thank-you notes for all the Christmas presents we received. We marveled at the flowers and sunshine in Pasadena while the snow fell outside our windows.

Need some ideas? Look up a holiday calendar online and

pick the ones that sound fun to you. Believe it or not, there's some sort of "holiday" for just about every day of the year! National Ice Cream Day (free cones at Ben & Jerry's), Pickle Day, Husband Appreciation Day (April 15), Clean Your Room Day (yes, it's true!). Pick one and start celebrating, or begin a tradition of your own.

Celebrations don't have to be overwhelming. By viewing them as opportunities to tell the stories of our families, we can relax from the pressure to do it bigger and better each year. As a result, celebrations can become cherished times for your family to remember those traditions, memories, and events that make your family special and unique.

Life is full of opportunities to celebrate. Pick one and go for it!

Remember the Sabbath day by keeping it holy.

EXODUS 20:8

A Simple Sabbath

MY MOTHER GREW UP EATING POT ROAST ON SUNDAYS after church, and she raised us on it, too. Pot roast in the slow cooker, surrounded by carrots, celery, potatoes, and onions cut in quarters. Fresh broccoli, thick gravy made with a *roux* in an iron skillet, and corn bread. For dessert, plum crisp with vanilla ice cream melting in the bottom of the bowl, or a chocolate Bundt cake with cherries.

We would walk in the door from the garage and be greeted by the homey smell, stomachs growling, mouths watering. A pastor and his family, a missionary couple from Africa, another church family, a grandmother needing company—there was always room at my mother's table.

We'd drop our Bibles in our rooms, kick off our Sunday shoes, and put on our slippers before heading to the kitchen to fill the glasses with ice and lemon slices, stir the iced tea, add the sprig of parsley to platters and serving bowls for decoration.

My mother always set the table the night before. Tablecloth, candles, cloth napkins. China, silver, and crystal. She never seemed to worry about our using her "good" china—she was confident that her children instinctively knew to be careful with beautiful things.

We stayed dressed in our Sunday best—the food seemed to taste better, we sat up straighter, remembered our manners more easily. And that way we matched the china, with its band of silver, and the sterling utensils from my parents' wedding.

Of course, there were seasons when we didn't eat pot roast. For example, we ate baloney sandwiches before going ice skating at the Air Force Academy. Sometimes we visited someone else's home for Sunday dinner.

But the Sunday dinner that means Sunday dinner to me is pot roast.

Sunday Dinner

It doesn't seem like people eat Sunday dinner together the way they used to.

Most often, our family goes out to brunch. We sit overlooking the ocean, eating eggs Benedict and drinking cup after cup of strong Italian coffee. Not bad, but not quite like I remember it.

My friend Bill is the king of Sunday dinner. While we tend to have company for dinner fairly often, Bill upholds Sunday afternoons as the best time for guests. I have to agree.

Listen to what chef and author Russell Cronkhite writes about the tradition of Sunday dinner:

Sunday dinner was once an American institution, a strong, familiar thread running deeply through our national fabric. I believe it can be that way again. A return to Sunday dinner can help bring us back to a time of craftsmanship, honor, values, and care. It can show us once again that time spent with those we love— enjoying family games, listening to tales of past struggle and glory, sharing our dreams and disappointments, and simply enjoying life together—far outweighs the amusements of the hectic, impersonal world that presses in all around us.... Sunday dinner is a gift we can give to one another and pass on to our children and our children's children. It's a much-needed respite of rest, celebration, and inspiration.[44]

On Sunday afternoons, children don't have to rush into the tub before bed. We're not yet worn out from a long day. Sunday afternoons have a rhythm all their own.

The problem is that sometimes we forget to listen.

We've gone to the opposite extreme of holiness when it comes to the Sabbath. Instead of setting Sunday apart as a day unlike any other, we've made Sunday a day *just like* any other. We run errands, do housework, finish homework projects—we catch up on all we've fallen behind in.

The Sabbath

Sabbath. The word sounds different, special somehow.

God created Sabbath for us—a day of rest, a day different than any other. Sabbath is a ritual that God Himself observed at Creation. As a commandment, it is the only one for which God uses Himself as the standard.

We're no longer living under the law, and we have escaped the numerous nitpicky rules set up by the Pharisees that Jews living in Jesus' day strained against. We are saved by grace—not by our strict observance of the command. As Jesus pointed out, the Sabbath was made for us, for our benefit. Have we abandoned something rich and rewarding just for another trip to the mall?

How do we take Sabbath in a world that never stops? When life moves on around us without slowing down for a rest, it's hard to imagine stepping back and resting as God desires. Women especially have difficulty taking time for themselves—there's too much to do, and we don't want to be selfish.

So how do we find Sabbath—for a day, for a moment? What does Sabbath look like, and how can we create a day of rest for our families?

The Old Testament is full of laws and information about the Sabbath. But they're all pretty simple, really. For example, "Remember the Sabbath day by keeping it holy."

So what is the Sabbath, and how do we keep it holy?

Sabbath began at Creation—or just after Creation, to be exact. "And God blessed the seventh day and made it holy, because on it he rested from all the work of creating that he had done" (Genesis 2:3). After completing the work of Creation, God took a day to cease work—to rest, to *enjoy* what He had put so much effort into. We rest on the Sabbath because God rested on the Sabbath. We follow His example.

In Exodus, the Sabbath became a sign and a covenant.

> Say to the Israelites, "You must observe my Sabbaths. This will be a sign between me and you for the generations to come, so you may know that I am the LORD, who makes you holy.... The Israelites are to observe the Sabbath, celebrating it for the generations to come as a lasting covenant." (Exodus 31:13, 16)

By the time Jesus was born, the Sabbath had remained a covenant, but there was little celebration to it. The focus was no longer on knowing God, but about following rules. In fact, there were hundreds of rules about how to keep the Sabbath. The Pharisees, or religious rulers, had organized these rules into thirty-nine categories of actions forbidden on the Sabbath, based on their interpretation of the Law and tradition.

The funny thing is, Jesus didn't comply with what the Pharisees thought was appropriate for the Sabbath. He grew up in a Jewish home and He certainly knew what was allowed and what was forbidden on the Sabbath day. Yet He healed people on the Sabbath and allowed His disciples to pick off heads of grain to eat when they were hungry on the Sabbath.

As God Himself, Jesus turned the accepted idea about the Sabbath on its head. He said, "The Sabbath was made for man, not man for the Sabbath" (Mark 2:27). The Sabbath isn't something we should have to endure or dread, like a root canal. God created the Sabbath for our benefit, for our enjoyment. The Sabbath is a day unlike any other—a day for rest and relaxation and fun and family and friends. The Sabbath is supposed to be a guilt-free vacation day each week—a day to not work and not feel guilty about not working. It is the one day not measured by how productive you were or how many things you checked off your to-do list.

Who couldn't use a day of vacation each week?

Celebrating the Sabbath

The Sabbath is a covenant to be *celebrated*. And so we're back once again to the idea of celebrating story.

I love the Sunday story that Pa tells Laura and Mary in *Little House in the Big Woods*. Sundays, he said, were very serious and solemn days for their grandfather. A long morning of sitting in church on hard pews for hours, and an even longer afternoon of sitting still in the parlor. Not much fun for energetic little boys.

So when their father fell asleep, the boys sneaked out of the house to try out their new sled, completed the night before and untested. They slid down the hill, picking up a pig along the way that got in the road. They flew down the hill, with the pig squealing all the way, and quietly sneaked back in the house—only to meet their father's stern gaze.

For Pa's father, Sundays were dreaded and fun was nowhere in sight.

I don't think dread was what God had in mind when He created the Sabbath. Why else would He have told us to *celebrate* Sabbath? Celebrations aren't dreary, dull, or demanding. Celebrations are fun! A celebration is something we anticipate, counting the days until it finally arrives.

We can make the Sabbath a day of refreshment for our families, or we can make it a day full of rules about what not to do. Take a look at this quote from *Friday Night and Beyond*:

> *Shabbat* for kids can either be hours of don'ts and can'ts... or hours of fun, excitement, family, and activity.
>
> The challenge, for parents, is to convey all that makes *Shabbat* special and enjoyable, while teaching in a positive way anything that might be construed as a restriction. When properly done (and it takes practice), *Shabbat* should become the best day of the week for kids, something they anticipate with excitement all week long.[45]

The author then lists two pages filled with ideas for how to make the Sabbath fun for kids.

That's how God wants us to view the Sabbath—as a gift we look forward to and anticipate each week. When it's over, He wants us to turn to each other and say, "I can't wait to do this again!"

In today's world, we don't live under the restrictive rules and burdensome regulations about the Sabbath that the Pharisees clung to. Nor do we abide by the solemn Sunday rules of the pioneer days.

But we still don't have it quite right, I think. Instead of keeping the Sabbath holy—set apart, different, special—we've made it a day like any other. We skip the rest God offers for a hodgepodge of last loads of laundry, trips to the grocery store, last-minute school projects. We fall into bed, feeling like we've almost caught up, and then wake up on Monday mornings tired, unrested, with another week ahead to somehow get through.

There has to be a balance in there somewhere.

Sunday Memories

Growing up, my parents were pretty serious about keeping the Sabbath holy. We didn't run errands, didn't do homework, didn't work. As a little girl, I remember my parents shutting their door and taking naps on Sunday afternoons. As a child in elementary school, Sunday afternoons for a season meant ice skating at the Air Force Academy.

But when I think back on Sundays during my childhood, I mostly think about the Sundays of junior high school, when my family lived in England.

Looking back, it's easy to tell if a memory happened on a Sunday. Sundays, Sabbath days, the Lord's Day, were different from any other day of the week.

Sundays were full—but felt wide open. Aside from the early morning rush of choosing the right outfit and getting my bangs to curl just so, Sundays moved more slowly than other days.

We went to a small church in the town of Harrogate, with wooden pews and old ladies who wore hats with feathers and flowers to service each week. We sang hymns out of hymnals that didn't have the music printed, only the words. Sunday school met in the parlor of the manse, the pastor's house next door, joined to the church hall in the basement by a funny little staircase, narrow and twisting.

After church we'd head to Eva's house. Eva was my mother's best friend when we lived in England—a beautiful woman who lit up when she smiled. And since she was always smiling, she glowed. She grew up on a farm and worked hard all her life. She had the gift of seeing God's hand in the smallest detail of the world around her.

Eva would make roast beef with Yorkshire puddings as big as your plate, baked in bread pans, and served as a separate course with gravy. We'd eat potatoes roasted brown and crisp on the outside, steaming hot and soft inside. Carrots, broccoli, and peas were passed around the table in big bowls.

Eva's table wasn't big enough to hold the crowd that always came. Her family of six, our family of four, another family or two, and a couple or two crowded around a makeshift table fashioned from sawhorses and boards, as well as the formal dining room table—all hidden beneath linen cloths. No matter how big the crowd, somehow we all managed to fit.

And there was always enough to eat. Looking back, it doesn't make sense; but I'm sure it was not unlike the widow's jar of oil, or the five loaves and two fish. God was present, and He made the table and the food sufficient.

After Sunday dinner, we'd pile in cars and head to the countryside to walk through green fields, climbing over stiles across stone walls. Think James Herriot in *All Creatures Great and Small*—that's where we lived! It sounds idyllic, and it was. But that's how people live. In fact, Toben and I went back to Yorkshire several years ago, and families were still out walking along country lanes on Sunday afternoons—in March, in the cold.

Our Sundays ended with another church service in the evening, followed by tea and digestive biscuits in the church hall. Instead of feeling busy and full and dull, Sundays were restful, fun, and wonderful.

I want Sundays like that for my family. I want the girls to grow up remembering Sundays as special days, a day different from all others.

Why is it so hard to make it happen?

Last Sunday we got part of it down. We missed church because Toben wasn't feeling well, and by the time everyone woke up and ate breakfast it would have been a mad rush to get to church, dressed and on time—not to mention in a happy frame of mind. We ended up running some errands—definitely not on my ideal Sunday plan.

But then we all went to the beach. We parked and walked across the bridge, before splashing in the river mouth and walking up the beach. Audrey and Emma chased seagulls and sandpipers, yelling "caw, caw" at the top of their lungs. They played at the water's edge while Toben and I wandered along, watching pelicans swoop and dive and glide along the surface of a wave. We found seashells and barnacles and a lobster tail.

My kids love the beach. They run ahead and draw pictures in the sand for us to find. They dance and sing and skip and jump and throw rocks and drag sticks in the sand to make lines that follow them wherever they go.

I held Toben's hand and thought, *I have to remember this moment—right now—forever.* Then Emma turned around quickly, hair wild and curly, and yelled, "This is so great! Isn't this great?"

We made it back to the car and picked up the girls to set them on the bumper. They sat there, grinning and laughing at the shoes of sand stuck to their feet.

It felt like Sunday.

We drove back home and everyone rested while the smell of dinner cooking filled the house. We watched a movie, laughing and singing along. I worked on a project; Toben napped on the couch. A friend came over for dinner and we sat in the dining room, lingering over our meal and talking "of shoes—and ships—and sealing-wax—of cabbages—and kings—," as the Walrus said.[46]

Definitely Sunday.

A Taste of the World to Come

I've been reading a fascinating book I found at the library about the Sabbath, called *Friday Night and Beyond: The Shabbat Experience Step-by-Step*. It's a guide for celebrating the Sabbath. I've enjoyed it so much that I ordered my own copy—so I can write in it to my heart's content.

In it, the author walks the reader through the Sabbath—each action, each blessing, each word—from preparation on Friday to the end of Sabbath on Saturday night, explaining what is done, when it is done, and why it is done.

I've learned all kinds of things—like that Sabbath is over when three medium-size stars are visible in the night sky, that each child receives a special blessing as part of the Sabbath meal on Friday night, and that Proverbs 31 is sung during the first Sabbath meal, often by the husband to his wife.

We ran into a Jewish friend at a party the other night, and I told him about all I had learned. Toben said I've gone completely *meshugana* and that he's worried I'm converting. But converting to Judaism isn't really necessary—as a believer, I'm Jewish by faith, and the traditions and ceremony of *Shabbat* are already mine for the taking.

I love this quote from the book:

When God announced that He was giving the Torah to the Jewish people, He said: "If you fulfill all these commandments, you will inherit heaven—the World to come."

The people asked: "Master of the Universe, won't you show us a sample of that World in THIS world?"

And so He replied: "Here is *Shabbat*. It will bring you a small taste of the pleasure and peace of the World to come."[47]

The Sabbath is supposed to be a taste of the world to come. Is that what my Sabbaths look like? Not usually. But I want this to be true and so I've committed not to work on Sundays, but instead to focus on my family, to take the time to rest, to read, to enjoy. I want to celebrate the Sabbath, to get back on track for the week to come.

Throughout our week it is easy to get caught up in our accomplishments and projects. It is a natural outcome of the extremely busy lives we lead. Thus, we were given a day to refocus and get back in touch with the meaning of it all and, most important, the Source of it all.... We enter *Shabbat* one way, and we leave another. When it is over, we have learned and grown, so that we can now give even more to our daily lives and to others.[48]

Shabbat is a rare and unique gift. Appreciating its beauty and understanding the depths of its wonder sometimes means seeing it in contrast to the rest of the week.

And *Shabbat* is a different plane. When it ends, it is not just that the clock has ticked away; it is that the level that we have enjoyed has also come to an end. For the week is not *Shabbat*. If we have used the *Shabbat* properly, however, we may be able to infuse some of it into our week.[49]

When we don't celebrate the Sabbath, we miss out on the opportunity to begin the new week with more, rather than less.

The kind of Sabbath day I want for myself and my family doesn't just happen. I've tried waking up on a Sunday expecting it to be something special, something different; but I've found that, as I go through the day, it just doesn't come together the way I hope it will. It takes work, planning, deliberate intention.

I was talking with my mother about this the other day. She reminded me that it's a process. I don't have to have it all figured out by the time next Sunday rolls around (which is good, because that's tomorrow!). We can try different things and see what works. For Sabbath to be a family thing, I'm going to have to get the whole family involved.

According to the Sabbath manual, "That which takes the most effort will, in the end, yield the greatest pleasure."[50] Effort must be put forth to create Sabbath. So what's it going to take?

I read somewhere that most people who like to write also love making lists. It's certainly true in my case! So, I ask again, what's it going to take?

Getting the family on board. Toben and I have to talk about how the Sabbath will work best for our family. Something tells me that we'll have very different ideas about this, but if the Sabbath is going to yield great pleasure for us, we need to start on the same page.

That means that Audrey and Emma need to learn why the Sabbath is important and why we may change how we do some things. If we're not going to watch television on a Sunday afternoon, they'll want to know why.

Preparation. What are our plans for the Sabbath this week? What time will we go to church? What do we want to do after church? Where are we going to eat? These simple questions all need to be answered before we roll out of bed on a Sunday morning. Knowing and making plans in advance for the Sabbath means that we're looking forward to the day, and that we won't waste time in the endless cycle of asking, "What do you want to do?" "I don't know. What do you want to do?" (Does your family do this? Or is it just us?)

Flexibility. I think in order for the Sabbath to work well, we've got to be flexible. While I want the structure and security of Sabbath tradition for my family, I don't want us to be rigid. We can try different things, and if it's not working, we can try something new.

The important thing is to try things that make the day different from any other. "The greatest tool we have for appreciating anything is the ability to distinguish and differentiate. When we see things are rare and unique, they stand out as special."[51]

Sunday Night Lunch

In the fifth book in the *Betsy-Tacy* series, we're introduced to Sunday night lunches at the Ray house.

> Sunday night lunch was an institution at the Ray house. They never called it supper; and they scorned folks who called it tea. The drink of the evening was coffee, which Mrs. Ray loved, and although Betsy and Margaret still took cocoa, their loyalty was to coffee for her sake.
>
> The meal was prepared by Mr. Ray. This was a custom of many years' standing. No one else was allowed in the kitchen except in the role of admiring audience. He

didn't object when Anna or Mrs. Ray made a cake earlier in the day; he didn't mind the girls putting a cloth on the dining room table. But in the kitchen on Sunday evenings he was supreme.

First he put the coffee on. He made it with egg, crushing shell and all into the pot, mixing it with plenty of coffee and filling the pot with cold water. He put this to simmer and while it came to a boil, slowly filling the kitchen with delicious coffee fragrance, he made the sandwiches....

Mr. Ray didn't mind company for Sunday night lunch; in fact, he liked it. The larger his audience, the more skill and ingenuity he displayed in his sandwich combinations. Tall, black haired, big-nosed, benevolent, an apron tied around his widening middle, he perched on a stool in the pantry with assorted guests all around.

The guests were of all ages. Friends of Mrs. Ray and himself...the High Fly Whist Club crowd...friends of Julia, Betsy and Margaret were equally welcome. Old and young gathered in the dining room around the table beneath the hanging lamp.... Talk flourished.[52]

After eating and sitting around the fire, Betsy's sister Julia played the piano and everyone sang the night away. What fun!

Okay, so maybe I'm not ready to make coffee with eggs, shells and all. Incidentally, why would one do this? Is it to add protein? To make it thick? Do you strain the coffee after it simmers? I asked my mom, thinking that maybe my grandmother had done it this way at one time, but she was as confused as I.

Furthermore, we don't own a piano, so that's out for now. But the phrases that jump off the page and grab my fancy are ones like "an institution in the Ray family," "guests were of all ages," "equally welcome," and "talk flourished."

I love that they had a tradition and that everyone loved it and was part of it. The *Betsy-Tacy* books are based upon the life of the author, Maud Hart Lovelace, and Sunday Night Lunch (in caps, no less!) was a Hart family tradition. She said:

> I loved to put down how many boys came to Sunday Night Lunch each week. You would think from my diary that they came to see me, but that was far from being the case. I wasn't the attraction. To this day when I meet some of those boys, grandfathers, now, of course, they look at me dreamily and say, "Oh Maud, I can still remember your father's onion sandwiches."[53]

Learning to Rest

I was reading Psalm 23 this morning and was struck once again by the idea that God "makes me lie down" in green pastures. It reminds me of how much I'm like a two-year-old no matter how old I get! When it was naptime, I always had to make Audrey lie down and go to sleep. It didn't come naturally for her to lie down. (Emma, on the other hand, still says "Yeah!" when she asks if it's bedtime and the answer is yes.)

Why does God make me lie down? Because on my own I'd lie down for about five minutes, and then I'd jump up to pull weeds, mow the grass, or talk to the other sheep. Can you relate? Do you sit down on the couch in the afternoon to rest, and then remember something you forgot to do? You jump up, put the clothes into the dryer, start another load in the washing machine, remember an e-mail you forgot to send, stop to unload the dishwasher, pick up a few toys. Then it's time to fold the laundry from the dryer and go to the bus stop to pick up the kids. Rest time is over.

God gets involved and has to "make me lie down" because rest must be taught; we must learn to rest.

Why doesn't rest come naturally? For me, it gets pushed down on the list, brushed aside for all of those things that seem more pressing.

But *rest is important*. God "makes me lie down" in those green pastures for the purpose of restoring my soul. And that's something I want—how about you? I think one of those ways God "makes me lie down" is by making "remember the Sabbath day by keeping it holy" a commandment. The Sabbath has the potential to restore my soul if I will only cooperate.

I was doing my Bible study homework the other morning and came across this definition for the Hebrew word *restore* in Psalm 23: "To turn back, to turn around, to return." It means going back to the point of departure and setting out again.

I love thinking about the Sabbath like this. The Sabbath is my chance every week to turn around, to turn back, to think again of the way I want to live, the way I want my family to function, the way I want to walk closely with my God. The Sabbath is my chance to return to God, to the point where I strayed from the path, and to begin again.

What a gift the Sabbath is when looked at like this! Instead of figuring out on my own how to get back on track by rejoining the path, the Sabbath returns me to where I veered off course so no part of the path is missed.

I love Jesus' words at the end of Matthew 11. In *The Message*, they read like this:

> "Are you tired? Worn out? Burned out on religion? Come to me. Get away with me and you'll recover your life. I'll show you how to take a real rest. Walk with me and work with me—watch how I do it. Learn the

unforced rhythms of grace. I won't lay anything heavy or ill-fitting on you. Keep company with me and you'll learn to live freely and lightly." (vv. 28–30)

Recover my life. Do you ever feel like your life has somehow gotten away from you, like a kite pulled by the wind? Somehow in the dips and turns, you've let go of the string and it's off flying here and there as the wind demands.

Sabbath is our time each week to come away with Jesus and recover our lives.

Sabbath is for our benefit, for our rest, for our refreshment. Sabbath is not heavy or ill-fitting, though we may have to take Jesus up on His offer to teach us how to take a real rest.

We learn, He says, as we walk with Him and keep company with Him. We learn from Him day by day. Because if we limit our relationship with Jesus to Sabbath alone, it quickly becomes religion and we burn out.

Sabbath Moments

I'm sitting at my dining room table, looking out the window into my backyard. It rained last night, and there are big puddles on the patio and putting green. It has just started to rain again, and watching the drops send out circles in the puddles is mesmerizing. Joey the cat is sitting by the sliding glass door, perfectly still and alert, watching with me. He's fascinated by the rain.

Why don't we stop and just watch the rain fall? Are we really too busy to notice what God is creating in each puddle?

Sabbath doesn't have to be limited to Sundays. I recently went through Beth Moore's study *Beloved Disciple: The Life and Ministry of John*, in which she talks about finding Sabbath moments—moments of rest and recreation in the midst of our busy lives.[54] This reiterated for me that while some Sabbath moments are scheduled—ballet class, lunch with a friend—others are spontaneous—pulling over to watch the waves for a few minutes, stopping for a latte when I need a pick-me-up.

The idea captured my attention, and I have begun to look for Sabbath moments throughout my day. Like taking the time to stop and breathe deeply. Or stopping to pay attention to the colors in the sky. Noticing the perfect bloom on my camellia bush when I walk outside. And acknowledging that it all comes from God.

Sabbath is a gift made just for us by the God who knows us better than we know ourselves. Sabbath is an oasis of peace, calm, and rest in the middle of our lives.

Defined this way, Sabbath is something I know I want and need for myself and for my family. What about you? Could you use some rest? Some peace for your family? Some time to be together and to set aside the worries and cares of living in today's world?

God offers you the opportunity to find what you're searching for. Week after week He holds it out to you. Don't you think it might be time to reach out and take it?

"There is no such thing as a common day.
Every day has something about it no other day has.
Haven't you noticed?"[55]

Simple Pleasures

SOMETIMES I AM AFRAID THAT I HAVE FORGOTTEN how to play. Or maybe the ability is there, but it's a little atrophied from lack of practice. I'm not sure when I stopped, but my memories of playing have grown fewer as the girls have gotten older.

Doesn't that seem backward to you? It does to me. It seems like I should play more with my children, not less. Yet here I am, minutes from the ocean—and the last time I really played in the sand was almost a year ago. Oh, I've been to the beach any number of times, but I haven't sat down in the sand, built a castle, flown a kite, or rolled my pants to my knees and splashed and danced and shouted with wild abandon. Things I used to do whenever I had the chance.

Why is that?

I suppose that with children I have become a grown-up. I have left the play to them, and have taken on the worries of sand in the car, the discomfort of wet clothes, the inconvenience of getting my hair wet, the concern of catching a cold.

Ugh.

I do find pleasure in my life—I dance, I knit, I spend time with my friends. But for the most part, those things are productive things. I dance to combat the Girl Scout cookies, I knit to make gifts, I spend time with my friends in Bible study or planning Brownie meetings.

I want to play for the sake of playing.

But I don't very often.

Too Easily Pleased

Our Brownie troop went on a camping trip not too long ago—cabin camping, that is. (Tent camping requires something like ten more hours of training and there are fifteen girls in our Brownie troop. Enough said.)

The camp we went to has the greatest playground. As I sat with the other mothers and talked, I was overcome with a desire to play. There was no laundry to fold, dishes to wash, floor to mop, or phone calls to make.

I went down the slide. It's huge—at least eighty feet high. Stairs, a ramp, and a ladder lead to the top of a very tall tree, from which you can see the whole world spread out below. And the slide is fast. I went down once, yelling "Wheeee!" all the way down and then grabbed Audrey to go down again. We made a train and whooshed down, our hands in the air, yelling and laughing when we landed in a pile at the bottom. We jumped up to do it again.

I swung on the rope swing, sitting on a little, round wooden disk. Another mom grabbed the rope's tail and swung me around and around, spinning faster and faster. I leaned back and watched the treetops careen above me.

I swung on the regular swings, pumping my legs back and forth, straining to soar higher and higher. Then I closed my eyes and flew.

Pure joy.

Why are we satisfied with the ordinary when incredible joy awaits? And why don't I seek it out more often?

C. S. Lewis once wrote that "we are far too easily pleased." Are you? Am I?

⌒

I want to be like David and dance with reckless abandon before the Lord, get caught up in the feel of the music, the joy of the moment, the feel of muscles stretching and straining.

Instead, I am more often like Michal, lofty and looking down, worried what others will think and say. Was she really concerned with what the people would think of a dancing, reckless, mad-with-joy king? Or was she caught off guard by the intense longing she had to join him—a longing that stole into her heart unannounced, yet was too great to ignore?

Slowing Down

Emma and I took the long way home from running errands the other day. We went down the beach rather than the freeway. The sun was high overhead, the sky was clear and so very blue.

We drove along in silence, looking out the window as much as was possible while driving at the same time. Really, I'm surprised there aren't more car accidents along our stretch of the 101. It's almost impossible not to look at the ocean while you're driving. After all, you never know when you'll spy a pod of dolphins.

"Why did God make the ocean, Mom?" Emma asked from the backseat.

"For His pleasure," I answered without pause.

For His pleasure. What does it mean that we are created in the image of God, who creates things for His own pleasure? Why else would God make those monkeys with red bottoms or ant-eaters or elephants? Why else would God make so many kinds of flowers, so many kinds of fish, so many colors?

Don't you wonder if God ever watches us rushing around and shakes his head saying, "Don't you *see* what I've made? Haven't you noticed?"

☙

I'm tired of rushing around. I'm tired of feeling like my days are too full and over in an instant, and that the only way to remember yesterday is to look at my to-do list and the things that didn't get done.

I'm tired of moving faster…and faster…and faster still.

I know I can't just yell, "Stop! I want to get off!" Life does go on. But I'm going to slow it down a little. I don't like moving so fast that I miss what's going on around me. I don't want to zoom past the roses on the highway going ninety miles an hour. It's not safe to stop on the highway to smell them. But it's probably a good idea to at least slow down so they're not a blur. The speed limit, after all, is only 55.

Despite all this rushing around, "I'm bored!" is something I hear more than I'd like to. What about you? It's one of those things that every mother has heard too many times to count. Dependence upon television, computer games, and too many toys to count has trained our children—and us, too, if we're totally honest about it—to expect to be entertained.

How do we get back to the simple pleasures of life? How do we say, like Oscar Wilde, "I adore simple pleasures"? We need to teach ourselves and our children to find joy in the simple things—a walk on the beach, climbing a tree, jumping rope, painting, knitting, kicking a soccer ball. We've fallen for the subtle lie that the more complex something is, the better it must be. How do we learn to turn off the television, to be comfortable with silence?

Many people believe that we are moving toward a time when we will have to make do with less. If we stripped away the excess in our lives, would we survive? How can we train ourselves to find contentment and a greater quality of life without so much stuff?

It often seems that we lose the ability to find joy in such simple pleasures as we grow up. I did. I worried more about what was cool, how I looked, when the next "big" thing was coming. I missed so many small moments because I was too busy looking ahead. This has always been a particular struggle of mine. My tendency is to look ahead rather than enjoying the moment I'm in.

As I choose simplicity in my daily life, I find that it's becoming easier to revel in the moment, to take joy in the simple pleasures that come with each day. I've learned to try new things without worrying about what others think. I take time throughout the day to stop and concentrate on the pleasure of the moment, to make a memory so I won't forget the joy I feel.

Making a Memory

Every once in a while I have a moment where I think, *I have to remember this for the rest of my life.* It always makes me think of Haley Mills in the original movie version of *The Parent Trap.* I've loved that movie since I was little—in fact, I used to dream about finding a long-lost twin sister and all the fun we'd have together.

There's a scene in the movie when one of the twins, Susan, meets her grandfather for the first time. She hugs him tightly and sniffs his collar.

"What are you doing, child?" he asks, a little alarmed.

"I'm making a memory," she responds matter-of-factly, "so that someday, when I'm quite grown up, I'll remember my grandfather and how he smelled of peppermints"—she pauses to sniff once more—"and pipe tobacco."

Susan knew that making a memory requires our focused attention. Maybe that's why it's called *making* a memory. We must stop and give our full attention. We have to engage our minds, our wills, and our senses. Like her, the memories I have come from simple things: the taste of a sun-warmed cherry straight off the tree; the perfect peach, eaten late one afternoon while sitting on my bicycle in a small town in Germany; my own grandfather's love of chalky pink peppermints.

Nineteenth-century French philosopher Marcel Proust also understood the idea of memory. In fact, he held forth the notion that the memory of something is truer than the thing itself. In *Remembrance of Things Past*, a cup of tea and a *petite madeleine* transport Proust back to his childhood:

> No sooner had the warm liquid, and the crumbs with it, touched my palate than a shudder ran through my whole body, and I stopped, intent upon the extraordinary changes that were taking place. An exquisite pleasure had invaded my senses.... Whence could it have come to me, this all-powerful joy?
>
> And suddenly the memory returns...in that moment all the flowers in our garden and in M. Swann's park, and the water-lilies on the Vivonne and the good folk of the village and their little dwellings and the parish church and the whole of Combray and of its surrounds, taking their proper shapes and growing solid, sprang

into being, town and gardens alike, from my cup of tea.[56]

Our senses—taste and smell—can take us back in time in an instant. Close your eyes for a moment and think about the flavor of freshly squeezed lemonade...the cool taste of a popsicle on a hot summer day...the sound of waves crashing on the shore...the feel of the sun warming your skin. You'll find yourself in another time, another place.

Some things we remember without prompting—graduations, weddings, first kisses. But to celebrate the everyday small things that make up the day-to-day fabric of our lives, we must do the work.

Write It Down

When I was pregnant with Audrey I found a wonderful journal that asked questions and prompted responses and thoughts about pregnancy. During those nine months, I grew so used to writing down the things I was feeling, the foods I craved, the gifts I received, that I couldn't give it up. "Dear Baby," they all began.

So after Audrey was born, I bought a big, black, blank journal and began writing letters to her. I recorded her achievements, her growing list of words, thoughts on her birthdays, and my feelings about first days of school.

When I found out I was pregnant for the second time, I headed to the bookstore on my way home from the doctor's office. "Dear Baby," I began.

Without a place and the intentional choice of writing down some of my memories, I might forever lose the fact that after going to the circus, Audrey used to run around the house singing, "Ladies and jungle men, boys and girls!" Or that Emma told me that she makes room in her heart for Jesus every night when she says her prayers. "That way," she explained, "He doesn't have to sleep on the floor."

How are you making and recording your memories? What are you doing to remember today? Nothing important has to happen—it could just be Thursday. But if you happen to be driving down the beach with your hair blowing in the breeze, smelling a tantalizing mixture of sea and Mexican food, singing your heart out along with the Indigo Girls—then it might be a good idea to stop and think, *I want to remember how this feels forever*.

Feel the sun on your face, take a deep breath, and hold it for a second. Let it out and continue on your merry way, knowing the memory is made and stored away for the next time it's cold and rainy and you're feeling blue.

☙

After I picked up Audrey from the bus this afternoon, we lay in her bed together and she read me a book about Olympic gold medalist Sarah Hughes (she calls her Sarah "Hugs").

We took turn reading paragraphs. The book described Sarah winning the gold medal and how her coach helped her record the moment: She put her hands on Sarah's shoulders, and then told her to close her eyes and take a deep breath. That, she said, would help her remember the feeling forever.

"Do you think that would work?" I asked Audrey.

"Maybe," she said.

So we tried it. We lay on top of the duvet, our heads on the patchwork pillows, and closed our eyes. We took a deep breath and held it for a minute. I concentrated on the feeling of Audrey lying in bed next to me, the sound of her voice. Then we let out our breath and opened our eyes.

"Now we'll remember this forever," Audrey said.

I hope so. I hope it becomes one of those memories "that stands out like a photograph," clear and crisp and in perfect detail.[57]

Flowers Just for Me

I stopped at the little corner vegetable and flower stand on Saxony Road one morning on my way home from ballet class. Sweaty and sore, I needed some tomatoes to make BLTs for lunch, and I knew they'd have fresh ones. And they did—locally grown, vine ripened, red, red tomatoes that were bigger than softballs and only a dollar a pound.

I wandered among the produce looking at artichokes and asparagus, freshly made salsa, and local avocados before heading over to the flower section. Flower buckets were arranged in a huge circle to form a pyramid on top. Each bucket was filled with a different kind and color of flower. Single stems of amazing texture and hue, all individually priced. There wasn't a store-bought bouquet in sight.

There's something about buying fresh flowers that feels out of the ordinary, even extravagant, to me. I love that the only purpose flowers serve is beauty—and temporary beauty at that.

I was drawn to flowers of the palest green, a few with a tinge of yellow or pink, but mostly a silvery, creamy green. I asked, and the girl behind the counter told me just to pick and choose, to create a bouquet just as I liked. What freedom and fun to create something exactly for me and suited to what I love.

I began with a stem of cockscomb—ordinarily red, but this one a velvety pale green with sunny yellow tips. The way it twists and turns reminds me of coral in a reef somewhere tropical.

Next, I picked a stem of green that was heavy with long strands of tiny flowers. Each heavy strand listed downward, too weary to stand upright. I added a stately rose—again in a pale, creamy green—that was just about to unfurl. It looks fuller than the typical rose, like God decided to pack twice as many petals into just one flower. The petals were tightly bound, as if ready to burst with the excitement of blooming fully.

Finally, I added a stem separating into eight or nine smaller stems, each with a bud of green—some closed up completely, others just starting to open. A delicate cream—like fresh butter—with a hint of green at the edges. And one last flower, a shy shade of pale pink. It stood out in the bunch of flowers I held—a little different from the rest, but beautiful in its individuality.

I took my flowers up to the counter, eager so show the cashier what I'd created. "May I finish it up for you?" she asked. As she worked, I asked her about the different flowers and she told me their names—which I promptly forgot as we admired each in its turn. She added a spray or two of something green, trimmed the stems, and wrapped my bouquet in brown paper and string.

I walked out into the clear blue sunshine of a warm September morning, a little surprised at the incredible joy I felt from something so simple. I rolled up the windows to protect my flowers, picked up my cell phone, and left messages for my two best friends. "It's me," I said. "I just called to tell you that I stopped to buy flowers for myself on my way home from ballet class. I think you should go do the same!"

Pink Tights and Tutus

I became a ballerina when I turned thirty. Turning thirty was a big deal for me—I decided that there's no time like the present to try new things and that if I didn't make some of my dreams come true, they never would.

I found a few girlfriends (the same crowd from Paris) who wanted to be ballerinas too, and together we signed up for a class. We took a field trip to the dance store and bought leotards, pink tights, ballet slippers, and little gauzy skirts to wrap around our waists. (Pink tights just aren't very flattering on most people—especially where they meet your leotard!)

I remembered a few of the basic positions from the summer I took ballet in the third grade, but for the most part I felt like a little kid learning something new. We pliéd, tendued, and grand jétéd across the floor. I tried to learn to twirl—something that mostly comes naturally until you have to do it a million times in a straight line without throwing up. Then it's important to spot your turns, and for some reason that's just beyond me.

Our class learned a dance and we performed in the spring dance recital—with all the little kids. We wore purple tutus and red lipstick and slicked our hair back into buns. We had a ball.

After our family moved to California, I found a new ballet class. I am always happy to wake up on Tuesday and Friday mornings and head off to class. What can I say? I love leg warmers!

Are you doing things each week that you love to do? Is there something you've always longed to do but have never tried? If so, do it!

Pajama Days

I am a pajama girl.

Not to sleep in, necessarily—if I wear them in bed they always end up tangled: the pant legs bunched up around my knees, the shirt twisted around my body, keeping me from rolling over when I want to.

I just got two new pairs of pajamas and I love them, love them, love them. The pair I have on right now are turquoise-y blue—Tiffany blue, I call it—and covered in bunches of strawberries: fruit, leaves, and blossoms. There are pockets on the front of the shirt, and the berries are bright red and shaped like hearts.

The other pair is pink and covered in pictures of poodles in Paris. Fluffy white French poodles, wearing clothes and visiting the Eiffel Tower, sitting outside at a café, or walking along a Parisian sidewalk or through a garden like the Bois de Boulogne. I can't decide which pair is my favorite. I suppose it depends on how hungry I am.

Now, I love clothes as much as the next girl, but I really love coming home at the end of a busy day and putting on my pj's. I usually do this on Fridays, after I've been at Brownies—those girls are so much fun, but they really wear me out! Last Friday I told my carload of Brownies that I was going to put on my jammies as soon as I got home. Because it was only 4:30, they thought I was a little crazy. But they're only in the second grade; they'll learn.

Even better than putting on pj's early is never taking them off! At our house, we call those days "Pajama Days," and we stay in our pj's all day long. We sit on the couch and watch *Little House on the Prairie*, or lie in bed reading, or just do normal things, like laundry and ironing and baking cookies.

The only tricky part is when it's time to go to the bus stop in the afternoon.

The Mystery of Each Moment

"There is only now," Thomas Merton once wrote. I take his words to mean that, while there are important things we must do—making dinner, laundry, taking the kids to the doctor—we have only this moment. How are we spending it?

All too often, I find myself off in the future somewhere, worrying about something involving tomorrow, next week, or next year that may never come to pass. I drive home and realize when I get there that I can't remember anything about the drive! (Kind of scary, huh?)

I want to live in the moment, to notice whatever God has for me at this very point in time, to discover and appreciate the joy in the task at hand. I want to open my eyes "wide in wonder and belief" (Matthew 6:22, *The Message*), to take childlike pleasure in the moment. I want to follow Jesus' instructions in Matthew 6:34: "Give your entire attention to what God is doing right now, and don't get worked up about what may or may not happen tomorrow" (*The Message*).

I want to remember that "each day can be lived unto itself, not lived for the yesterday that is gone or for the tomorrow that may not come, but lived for this present moment in the presence of God."[58] Or, to rephrase it, "Each *moment* can be lived unto itself, not lived for the *moment* that is gone for the *moment* that may not come, but lived for this present moment in the presence of God."

Mark Buchanan puts it another way:

Pay attention to how God is afoot in the mystery of each moment, in its mad rush or maddening plod. He is present in both. But too often, we are so time-obsessed that we take no time to really notice.[59]

I don't want to be time-obsessed. I was reading blogs the other day and came across this entry written by a mom in Austin, Texas:

I'm surrounded by clocks, but I don't care what time it is. For the most part, Bea and I live our life like cats. We get up when we are done sleeping. We sleep when we are tired. We eat when we are hungry. We play the rest of the time.[60]

I'm so drawn to the simplicity of living life like this. Of listening to the moment and following its lead.

I want to be content in the now—whatever it brings.

Laura Ingalls Wilder once wrote, "I am beginning to learn that it is the sweet simple things of life which are the real ones after all."

What are the sweet simple things in your life? Are you rushing past them, taking them for granted? Or are you stopping to pay attention, to realize that these little things are the most real things of your life?

When I think of sweet simple things, the first that spring to mind are my children. Oh, they're getting big so fast. They lie under their covers at night, long and lean, and I realize that the dimples on their elbows and the rolls at their knees are gone and aren't coming back.

We've got to slow down. We can't just sit back and be carried along at the frantic pace of the world around us. It moves too quickly! We must choose to slow down, to notice the sweet simple things in our lives and to see God's presence in them. We must choose to enjoy the moment; to remember it, to hold on to its shape, its smell, its texture.

We must pay attention to the seasons
that surround us and we must live the
season in which we find ourselves.[61]

Changing Seasons

MY MOTHER HAS ALWAYS TALKED ABOUT LIFE IN terms of seasons. And I love the idea. While it felt like Audrey would never sleep through the night—and it did take about eighteen (long!) months—eventually she did, because it was just a season and seasons do change. It felt too like Emma would never get potty training down, but she did, because it was just a season.

I don't want to be a person who can "tell time, but not discern seasons," as Mark Buchanan says:

For only those who number their days aright gain a wise heart. Only they become God's sages: those calm, unhurried people who live in each moment fully, savoring simple things, celebrating small epiphanies, unafraid of life's inevitable surprises and reverses, adaptive to change yet not chasing after it.[62]

How I want to be like this! What about you?

Keep Trying

It's a constant struggle to choose to let go, relax, and have fun. So much of what we worry about, obsess over, and try with all our might to control is just not that complicated or even important. As we slow down, take our time, and take a step back to make a choice for simplicity, life unwinds a little, the pressure eases up, and joy returns.

Too often we allow ourselves to be stifled by the complexities of daily life. But we do have a choice, and we can simplify in search of a better quality of life. Take the phone off the hook, put the kids to bed early, and run a bubble bath. Leave the dirty dishes in the sink, turn up the music, and dance around the house with your kids.

It takes time and some trial and error to find what works best for your family. There's no special formula or secret recipe for the simple life. What works for your family this year might not work so well next year. As my mother says, there are seasons to life. The key is to be flexible, be willing to try new things, and try something else if it doesn't work.

The key is to keep trying.

Here's this idea again: Some of the things that regulate our lives are things that we can choose or change. Some are not. What is important is that we look at them from time to time and recognize which things are which, and which things can or should or might be adjusted in ways that help us to balance our lives.[63]

And as we seek a simple life we seek God first, knowing He'll help us figure it out, for He promises, "Seek the kingdom first, and everything else will come in due season."[64] As the seasons change, we realize that it is always the season to seek God.

There's no perfect recipe for living simply. What is simple and works for my family may not work for yours. You know your family and you know what's best for them. There's no one-size-fits-all simple life.

The point is to choose wisely—to know what you're choosing for your family, and why. Left without check, the world—your friends, your family, your kids' school, your church—will pile on more and more until you're buried with so many things, toys, and commitments that you find it hard to breathe. And not all of it is bad. But you only have so much time, so much energy, so much money, so many years with children at home.

Learning to Listen

I have recently begun to pray the morning office—called *Lauds*—each day. There's something wonderful about praying a service that people all over the world are praying and have been praying together for so long. I love the tradition of it, the ritual of it, the rhythm of it. The sameness of praying the office daily is not boring, nor is it done by rote. Instead, there is comfort and joy in the familiarity of repeating the same words each morning.

I suppose it could be possible to learn the prayers by heart, to say them from memory while thinking through my day—what to pack in the girls' lunchboxes, what to wear, the things I'd like to get done that day. But I have found such incredible depth and meaning to the reading aloud the words printed on the page.

Part of the prayer is called the *Venite*—Latin for "come"—the invitation to prayer. This is Psalm 95, which ends in my prayer book with these words:

We will know your power and presence this day,
if we will but listen for Your voice.[65]

If. Such a small word, yet it makes all the difference here: "*If* we will but listen for Your voice."

Listening makes me think of my children. I might tell one to do something—"Emma, go brush your teeth"—and she doesn't move. Sitting on the floor and watching television, she hears the sound of my voice, but she doesn't respond. "Emma!" I say, a little louder this time. She looks at me quickly, before turning back to the television once again. "Emma!" I say for the third time. This time I go and stand in front of the television, or pick up the remote and switch it off.

"Mom! I was watching that!"

For her to really listen to me, the distraction of television has to be dealt with; I must get down to her level and look in her face. Once her attention is focused on me, she can listen and obey.

I think I'm a lot like Emma sometimes. God speaks and I recognize that He said something, but I'm more focused on the distraction in front of me; His voice barely registers. He calls my name again and I turn for a moment, but then whatever it was in front of me pulls my attention back again.

Sometimes, God will deal with the distraction for me—turning off the television and getting down in front of me, turning my face toward His.

But other times, I think God is waiting for me to deal with it myself. To see Him and choose Him above whatever else is pulling at my attention. That's part of growing up, I think.

For now, I remind Audrey of her homework and help create space for her to get it done. I decide that it's time to do homework now. I remove the distractions; I sit down with her and help her work through her assignments. That's my job as the mother of a second grader.

But when she's in high school, it will be her own job to deal with distractions and focus on what she needs to do.

I don't know about you, but, despite being a "grown-up," I still have a hard time with some of those distractions on my own. The distractions in my life don't feel like something as simple as television. They are often worthwhile things, things that seem important, things that *are* important—to me. They aren't bad things, or even worthless things.

But the question has become, *Are those things more important than hearing God's voice when He speaks to me?*

Living Wide Open

I want to know God's power and presence this day. But in order to do that, I need to live more simply. I need to get rid of some of the things that fill up my life. I need to make more space in which I can sit up and listen to what God is saying to me.

The Gospel lesson for day 23 of whatever month it happens to be ends like this: "Pay attention to how you listen to Me."

This got me thinking about how I listen to God. Am I listening with just one ear—hearing the sound of His voice but not really paying much attention to the words themselves? Am I giving Him my full attention, watching intently to pick up on every gesture, every change in tone? Am I listening responsively? Am I listening with the intent of obeying? Or am I listening because I should, but really thinking of something else? Have I stopped what I'm doing to focus on Him alone? Am I charging ahead with what I think He's said, or am I asking questions to clarify so that I can understand fully?

So many questions. And I suppose the answers depend much upon the day, what's going on in my life, how hungry I am, whether the girls are awake yet, and so on.

But no matter the circumstances, I can make certain choices that will affect those answers, choices that will help me pay attention to how I'm listening and to listen better.

I can choose to make some space to listen, to get up when the house is still quiet, to read God's Word, to pray, to listen for Him to speak to me. I can make listening a priority, and I can ask God to help.

I must say no to some things, get rid of some other things, clear out some stuff. Isn't it amazing that choosing less in this way doesn't leave my life empty and lonely and dull? Isn't it amazing that it can be filled with God's abundance? The kind of abundance that doesn't leave me feeling crowded and pressed down and cramped and uncomfortable. That, instead, those spaces created are "wide open," as Paul writes in 2 Corinthians:

> I can't tell you how much I long for you to enter this wide-open, spacious life. We didn't fence you in. The smallness you feel comes from within you. Your lives aren't small, but you're living them in a small way. I'm speaking as plainly as I can and with great affection. Open up your lives. Live openly and expansively! (2 Corinthians 6:11–13, *The Message*)

It's like in Narnia, when they all find themselves inside the stable at the end of *The Last Battle*. There's a whole world inside, "Narnia within Narnia..." And Mr. Tumnus explains, "The further up and the further in you go, the bigger everything gets. The inside is larger than the outside.... [It's] like an onion: except that as you continue to go in and in, each circle is larger than the last."[66]

I love the idea of living wide open. God himself lives in wide-open space. In Psalm 118:5, David says, "I called to GOD; from the wide open spaces, he answered" (*The Message)*. To be where God is—that is to be in wide-open space.

And when He rescues us, God brings us to Himself—in that wide-open space. "He stood me up on a wide-open field; I stood there saved—surprised to be loved!" (Psalm 18:19, *The Message*). The Promised Land of Canaan was filled with wide-open space for the people of God:

> And now I have come down to help them, pry them loose from the grip of Egypt, get them out of that country and bring them to a good land with wide-open spaces, a land lush with milk and honey. (Exodus 3:8, *The Message*)

But we fill up that wide-open space with stuff, with rules, with anything and everything. Instead of enjoying the space for its space, we see it as a void to be filled. Why is that? Why do we place such value on being busy?

Why do we feel important when people ask us about our day and we fill them in on the laundry list of things to do, the double-booked appointments on the calendar, the "I'm just too busy" mantra? Conversely, why do I feel a little guilty when a friend asks about my day and I admit it's wide open?

I'm sitting in the library at my daughter's elementary school having just dropped off my mother for the grandparents' day program. I have an hour to kill, so I thought I'd sit someplace quiet and write. On my way out of the chapel, I ran into a friend I haven't seen in a while.

"I miss seeing you at Bible study," I told her.

Her work schedule and life schedule are full—and she said she doesn't have the time right now. "Why do I do this to myself?" she asked. "I make promises to myself not to overcommit and then I go and do it anyway."

Why, indeed? It can be hard enough to say no to things we don't want to do or know for sure we don't have time to do. But it's harder still to say no to things we want to do—volunteer at school, teach Sunday school, participate in Bible study, spend time with a friend.

And so God repeatedly draws us back to the wide-open space where we can meet with Him and where there's room for God to fill us with His presence. As Job's friend Elihu said, "Don't you see how God's wooing you from the jaws of danger? How he's drawing you into wide-open places—inviting you to feast at a table laden with blessings?" (Job 36:16, *The Message*).

As I cut back, as I simplify, as I create space, and as I walk into God's wide-open space, it's hard not to fill it back up. It's a challenge not to take on new commitments, to refuse to feel guilty because there's an empty day. But to sit back and rest and wait for God to fill that day as He chooses is a gift beyond measure.

'Tis the gift to be simple,
'tis the gift to be free,
'tis the gift to come down
where we ought to be,
and when we find ourselves in the place just right,
'twill be in the valley of love and delight.
When true simplicity is gained
to bow and to bend we shan't be ashamed,
to turn, turn, will be our delight
till by turning, turning we come round right.[67]

P. S.

I'VE JUST FINISHED GOING THROUGH THE LAST CHAPTER of this book, making changes suggested by my editor. And I have to laugh because in the past ten days, we've found ourselves facing a new season in our life.

Toben's job is changing and we're moving back to Colorado in the next six weeks. I say "we've found ourselves" because even though we're choosing to make the move, the decision happened so suddenly that it's easy to feel like we've been taken by surprise.

I have mixed feelings about going. I have loved living here in Southern California—despite all the excess and overload that sometimes makes this part of the country feel like a whole other world. I have made wonderful friends here—and it breaks my heart to think of leaving them and living my day-to-day life far away from their encouragement, their laughter, and their kindred-spirit-ness. And I've gone through hard times here—

times that have stretched me and broken me and made me stronger. In suffering I have found a dependency and reliance upon God that I've always longed for.

At the same time, I'm excited to live near my family again. My sister and her family have been visiting for the past week, and I have loved spending so much time with them. I'm excited to see my niece grow and change on a daily basis, and to continue to develop a real friendship with my sister as adult women, rather than as bickering siblings. And I'm thrilled beyond words to have my kids once again see their grandparents almost every day. I'm looking forward to Sunday dinners (pot roast, of course!) around each other's tables, birthday parties that include all our family, and dropping by whenever we happen to be in the neighborhood.

So here we are, simplifying again. As we get ready to put the house on the market we find ourselves sorting through clothes and toys and books, determining what will move with us and what we'll get rid of. We're talking about houses and figuring out the smallest house we can comfortably live in, asking again what we really need.

I'm making lists of the things that need to be done, the phone calls to be made, and stopping to remind myself to focus on the moment, to pay attention to those things that matter most, to listen to God as He directs our paths in this new season of our life together.

My Favorite Resources for Simple Living

Books

Nonfiction

Between the Dreaming and the Coming True by Robert
  Benson

Living Prayer by Robert Benson

A Good Life by Robert Benson

Venite by Robert Benson

Feeding Your Soul by Jean Fleming

Practicing the Presence of God by Jan Johnson

Walking on Water: Reflections on Faith and Art by Madeline
  L'Engle

Friday Night and Beyond: The Shabbat Experience Step-by-Step
  by Lori Palatnik

A Return to Sunday Dinner by Russell Cronkhite

A Family Guide to the Biblical Holidays by Robin Scarlata and
  Linda Pierce

The Holy Wild by Mark Buchanan

Fiction

Betsy-Tacy (and the rest of the series) by Maud Hart
  Lovelace

Emily of New Moon (and the rest of the series) by Lucy Maud
  Montgomery

Anne of Green Gables (and the rest of the series) by Lucy
Maud Montgomery
The Secret Garden by Frances Hodges Burnett
The House at Pooh Corner by A. A. Milne
Little Women by Louisa May Alcott
Little House on the Prairie (and the rest of the series) by Laura
Ingalls Wilder

Magazines

Real Simple
Martha Stewart Living
Cookie
Martha Stewart Kids

On the Web

For holiday ideas for almost every day of the year:
www.brownielocks.com
For ideas to simplify everyday life:
www.realsimple.com
For inspiration, recipes, holidays, and great ideas:
www.marthastewart.com
For filling your freezer with home-cooked meals:
www.dreamdinners.com
For recipes that use what you happen to have in the pantry:
www.epicurious.com

On CD

The Night of the Child from Upper Room Books: thoughts
and readings on the season of Advent

About the Author

Joanne Heim is the coauthor (with her husband, Toben) of *Happily Ever After: A Real-Life Look At Your First Year of Marriage* (NavPress, 2000, 2004), *Mosiaxstudy.com/Community* (NavPress, 2001), *Mosaixstudy.com/Men&Women* (NavPress, 2001) and *What's Your Story? An Interactive Guide to Building Community* (Piñon Press, 1999). She has also written or ghostwritten a number of Bible studies and study guides.

She has been a guest on numerous radio programs, including "Focus on the Family" with Dr. James Dobson, Moody's "Midday Connection," and "Life on the Edge—LIVE" by Focus on the Family. She has also been featured in many publications, including *Bridal Guide* and *Marriage* (Marriage Encounter).

She first noticed her husband in her ninth-grade algebra class, and they began dating when she was sixteen. When Toben proposed the night before she graduated from high school, she said, "YES!" They attended Whitworth College in Spokane, Washington, and got married in 1991. Joanne graduated in 1993 with degrees in Communication Studies and French, thrilled that the all-nighters associated with being the editor-in-chief of the school newspaper were over.

After a summer working in Paris for a French software company and learning that just a slight mispronunciation can change the meaning of a word, she began working for NavPress Publishing Group as a publicist before becoming the senior copywriter and a project editor.

When their first daughter, Audrey, was born in 1998, Joanne retired from full-time work, and began driving a minivan upon the arrival of their second daughter, Emma, in 2001. Since then, she has given up the van (not quite her!) and taken up ballet (definitely her!). She teaches women to knit each week during the school year and can often be found at the bus stop each afternoon knitting a Christmas present or helping someone pick up a dropped stitch.

You can read about her adventures in living a simple life each day at www.thesimplewife.typepad.com.

Notes

1. Robert Benson, *Between the Dreaming and the Coming True: The Road Home to God* (New York: Jeremy P. Tarcher/Putnam, 2001), 88.

2. Robert Benson, *Living Prayer* (New York: Jeremy P. Tarcher/Putnam, 1998), 71.

3. Ibid., 41.

4. From an MSN.com article, "Slow Down," http://lifestyle.msn.com/MindBodyandSoul/PersonalGrowth/ArticleMC.aspx?cp-documentid=454036 (accessed June 12, 2006).

5. John Michael Talbot, *The Lessons of St. Francis* (New York: Dutton Publishers), 24.

6. Maud Hart Lovelace, *Betsy Was a Junior* (New York: HarperTrophy, 1979), 166.

7. Robert Benson, *A Good Life: Benedict's Guide to Everyday Joy* (Brewster, MA: Paraclete Press, 2004), 38.

8. "Prayer for Serenity," attributed to Reinhold Niebuhr.

9. Benson, *Living Prayer*, 81.

10. Benson, *Between the Dreaming and the Coming True*, 88.

11. L. M. Montgomery, *Anne of the Island* (New York: Bantam Books, 1992), 81.

12. J. Howard Payne, "Home, Sweet Home," from the opera *Clari, the Maid of Milan*.

13. L. M. Montgomery, *Anne's House of Dreams* (New York: Bantam Books, 1992), 88.

14. L. M. Montgomery, *Emily Climbs* (New York: Bantam Books, 1993), 101.

15. Lovelace, *Betsy's Wedding* (New York: HarperTrophy, 1996), 221.

16. L. M. Montgomery, *Emily's Quest* (New York: Bantam Books, 1993), 82.

17. Ann Spangler, *Praying the Names of God* (Grand Rapids, MI: Zondervan, 2004), 180.

18. Lori Palatnik, *Friday Night and Beyond: The Shabbat Experience Step-by-Step* (Lanham, MD: Rowman & Littlefield Publishers, Inc., 2004), 3.

19. Truman Capote, *The Grass Harp* (New York: Vintage, 1993).

20. Laura Ingalls Wilder, *Little House in the Big Woods* (New York: Harper & Row, 1971), 29.

21. Amy Grant, "Softly and Tenderly," from the album *Legacy... Hymns & Faith* (Nashville: Word Entertainment, 2005). Adapted from a hymn written by Will L. Thompson in 1880, based on Mark 10:49, http://library.timelesstruths. org/music/Softly_and_Tenderly/.

22. C. S. Lewis, *The Last Battle* (New York: Collier Books, 1970), 171.

23. Madeleine L'Engle, *Walking on Water: Reflections on Faith and Art* (Colorado Springs, CO: Shaw, 1980, 1998, 2001), 198.

24. Beth Moore, *The Patriarchs: Encountering the God of Abraham, Isaac, and Jacob* (Nashville, LifeWay Press, 2002), 83.

25. Benson, *Living Prayer*, 72.

26. L'Engle, *Walking on Water*, 114.

27. Lovelace, *Betsy and Joe* (New York: HarperTrophy, 1979), 106.

28. Lovelace, *Betsy-Tacy* (New York: HarperTrophy, 1979), 14.

29. Lewis to Arthur Greeves, 29 December 1935, in *They Stand Together: The Letters of C. S. Lewis to Arthur Greeves, 1914–1963*, ed. Walter Hooper (New York: Macmillan, 1979).

30. Benson, *Living Prayer*, 141, 147.

31. Stormie Omartian, *The Power of a Praying Parent* (Eugene, OR: Harvest House, 1995), 70–71.

32. Benson, *Living Prayer*, 139.

33. Benson, *A Good Life*, 39.

34. Virginia Woolf, *A Room of One's Own* (New York: Harvest Books, 1989).

35. Lovelace, *Betsy's Wedding*, 245.

36. From *Youthworker Journal*, Nov/Dec 2005.

37. L. M. Montgomery, *Rainbow Valley* (New York: Bantam Books, 1992), 26.

38. Helen Treyz Smith, "Company Once a Week," *Better Homes and Gardens*, March 1937.

39. Ibid.

40. Lovelace, *Betsy's Wedding*, 136.

41. "I Love to Tell the Story," a hymn by A. Katherine Hankey, 1866.

42. From the *Oxford American Dictionary*, ed. Eugene H. Ehrlich et al. (New York: HarperCollins, 1982).

43. Melody Carlson, *Benjamin's Box* (Grand Rapids, MI: ZonderKidz, 2000), 27.

44. Russell Cronkhite, *A Return to Sunday Dinner* (Sisters, OR: Multnomah Publishers, 2002), 6–7.

45. Palatnik, *Friday Night and Beyond*, 79–80.

46. Lewis Carroll, from "The Walrus and the Carpenter," in *Through the Looking-Glass*.

47. Palatnik, *Friday Night and Beyond*, xiv.

48. Ibid., 89.

49. Ibid., 71.

50. Ibid., 89.

51. Ibid., 89.

52. Lovelace, *Heaven to Betsy* (New York: HarperTrophy, 1996), 112–115.

53. Ibid., 338, 341.

54. Beth Moore, *The Beloved Disciple: The Life and Ministry of John* (Nashville, LifeWay Press, 2002), 155.

55. L. M. Montgomery, *Anne of Ingleside* (New York: Bantam Books, 1992), 17.

56. Marcel Proust, *Remembrance of Things Past,* trans. C. K. Scott Moncrieff, Vol. 1 (New York: Random House, 1924), 34–36.

57. Lovelace, *Betsy Was a Junior,* 64.

58. Benson, *A Good Life,* 28.

59. Mark Buchanan, "Schedule, Interrupted," *Christianity Today*, February 2006, http://www.christianitytoday.com/ct/2006/002/29.43.html.

60. From a blog entry found on happythings.typepad.com.

61. Benson, *Living Prayer,* 59.

62. Buchanan, "Schedule, Interrupted."

63. Benson, *A Good Life,* 38.

64. Robert Benson, *Venite: A Book of Daily Prayer* (New York: Jeremy P. Tarcher/Putnam, 2000), 245.

65. Benson, *Venite*, 8.

66. C. S. Lewis, *The Last Battle*, 180.

67. Joseph Brackett, "Simple Gifts," a Shaker song written in 1848.

Look for other
Bliss books for women
at a bookstore near you.

Girl on a Swing

by Nancy Kennedy

☙

Lipstick Grace

by Nancy Kennedy (March 2006)

☙

God Is Not Through with Me Yet

by Thelma Wells (March 2006)

bliſſ Uncommon Refreshment *for* Women

www.mpbooks.com

Multnomah